quick & clever instant cards

quick & clever
instant cards

Julie Hickey

David and Charles

To the memory of my dad, Alf and to my father-in-law Laurie. You both always believed in me and encouraged me to reach for my goals. I know you would both have been so proud of me. Thank you. Julie x

A DAVID & CHARLES BOOK
David & Charles is a subsidiary of F+W (UK) Ltd.,
an F+W Publications Inc. company

First published in the UK in 2005

Distributed in North America
by F+W Publications, Inc.
4700 East Galbraith Road
Cincinnati, OH 45236
1-800-289-0963

ISBN 0 7153 2090 4 paperback

Printed in China by SNP Leefung
for David & Charles
Brunel House   Newton Abbot   Devon

Executive Editor Cheryl Brown
Editor Jennifer Proverbs
Art Editor Prudence Rogers
Text Editor Carey Denton
Photographer Ginette Chapman
Production Controller Ros Napper

Visit our website at www.davidandcharles.co.uk

David & Charles books are available from all good bookshops; alternatively you can contact our Orderline on (0)1626 334555 or write to us at FREEPOST EX2 110, David & Charles Direct, Newton Abbot, TQ12 4ZZ (no stamp required UK mainland).

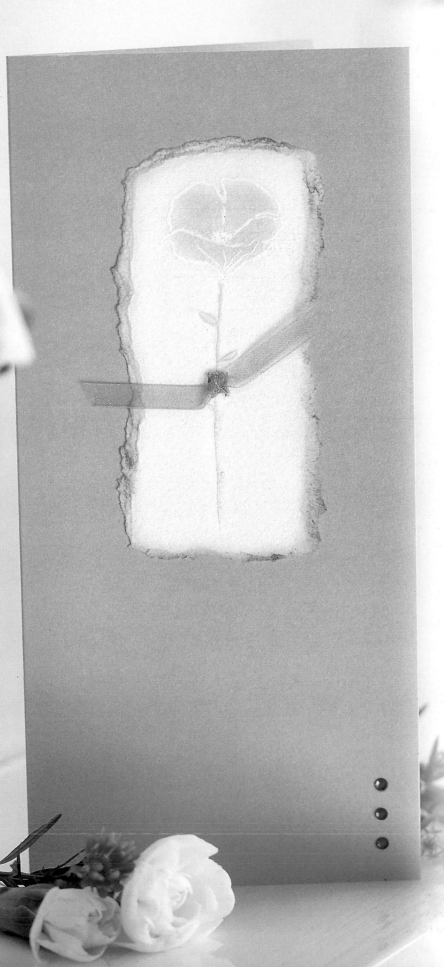

Contents

Introduction

In our busy and hectic lives the one thing we are all short of is time. But this doesn't mean we have to sacrifice the things we enjoy doing – like making greetings cards. This book is full of clever ideas for creating unique handmade cards in less time than it takes to go out and buy one. These pages are packed full of inspirational ideas for simple yet stylish cards and, just as importantly, the book will help you get organized so that when you want to make a card you have all that you need right there at your fingertips.

The first section of the book explores all the beautiful materials and clever equipment that is available and outlines some essential techniques for getting the best out of them for speedy and effective results. The second part of the book provides a wealth of card designs that you are sure to enjoy making, all of which can be made in just three easy steps.

Get organized

The key to 'instant' cards is to prepare in advance and collect the tools, equipment and materials you need for the type of cards you want to make. There are many fabulous ready-made embellishments on the market today, and if you combine them with gorgeous card and paper the results are sure to impress. A few well-chosen materials are all that you need: often the more simple and uncluttered the card, the more stylish the result.

It makes sense when buying your paper and card, card making accessories and other materials to think in themes. I like to build up a collection of materials for different categories: female family members and friends; children; men. Then, when I want to make a card for my brother, for example, I have items to hand that I can use and I don't have to go out and start looking. The

sections on embellishments and paper and card (see pages 16–23) give plenty of ideas for buying and using some of these wonderful materials.

Easy as 1, 2, 3!

In the 16 project chapers I show you how to create simple yet stylish cards in next to no time, and I've suggested clever ideas to cover every occasion. Each project is completed in only three steps, making them fast, fuss-free and ideal when time is short.

Be inspired

Each card project is accompanied by three alternative design ideas, inspired by a themed collection of materials. You will see how I arrange all the elements on the card so that they work together to create a harmonious whole. I take my inspiration from all sorts of places, but especially home furnishing departments where

cushions, handbags, rugs, wallpaper and fabric are all sources of creative ideas. It's easy for you too to take inspiration from all around and collect card-making materials to reflect themes you see and occasions you celebrate, ready to be quickly combined at a moment's notice. Plus I've included handy ideas for greetings to write inside your handmade cards to make them suitable for all occasions.

I hope you will all take inspiration from my book, but also feel free to change or adapt any of the card designs: add your own style, combine bits from several cards, but above all make them yours – in an instant!

Enjoy

Julie

Get Ready

Equipment

Organization is the key to producing creative cards quickly. A store of tools and equipment will ensure that you are able to get to work as soon as you have an idea, and choosing the right storage option will ensure you can find what you need, when you need it. You don't have to buy expensive tools straightaway, but a basic tool kit of equipment that you will use again and again is essential.

Quick & Clever

There are lots of wonderful decorative tools and equipment to choose from – keep them safe and organized in a sturdy storage box, such as a DIY tool box or a specialist craft storage system.

Basic tool kit

Every project lists the specific materials you need; in addition you will always need items from this kit, so make sure you always have it on hand. See pages 14 and 15 for more about adhesives.

Cutting mat This is the best surface for cutting on with a craft knife as the mat is self-healing and the cut marks seal back up. It also provides a firm, flat surface to rubber stamp on.

Craft knife Use to cut out awkward shapes, trim pieces of card down to size and to help stick small stickers on to cards. Always use a sharp blade.

Metal ruler An essential piece of equipment for cutting straight lines with a craft knife.

Plastic ruler For measuring card and paper.

Set square Use this to align work centrally on cards. There is a centre '0' position with centimetre or inch markings worked out from this point to the left and right. Mark the centre of your card. Position the centre '0' of the set square on this mark and then use the measurements on either side to position different elements of the card precisely.

Double-sided tape Perfect for mounting card or paper on to card.

Glue pen The fine nib makes this perfect for sticking on small shapes.

All purpose sticky craft glue A good, all-round strong adhesive.

Adhesive foam pads Sticky on both sides, they are great for achieving a raised effect.

Pencil Use to trace patterns, mark measurements and countless other little jobs.

Eraser Use a clean plastic eraser, as it is important not to leave marks on the card.

Scissors Fine-pointed scissors will enable you to get right into the nooks and crannies. Soft foam handles are very comfortable to use.

Tracing paper Use to trace off patterns provided at the back of the book (see pages 106–108) or from other sources.

Bone folder This is a vital piece of equipment for the card maker as it creates perfect creases and professional-looking cards.

Guillotines

This is an essential tool: it is much easier to achieve a straight line with a guillotine than a craft knife and it gives a professional finish. They come in different sizes to deal with different sized card and some have decorative blades. You may want to invest in at least one if you become a keen card maker. To stop the paper moving, always push your card against the back edge and hold the plastic shield down firmly while using the blade.

Specialist tools

There are many specialist tools that, although not required for every card, are great fun to try. They may be an initial investment but will help you produce professional results and save you a great deal of time. I have built up my workbox over a number of years, and still enjoy adding to it today!

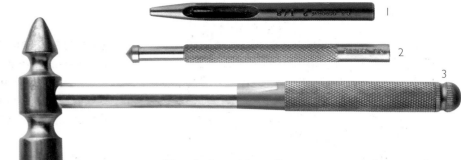

Eyelet setter, hammer and punch

Use with eyelets and snaps: setter and punch come in different sizes to match. Make a hole with the punch (1), insert an eyelet or snap, turn the card over and use the setter tool (2) and hammer (3) to flatten the eyelet or snap and attach it to your card. (See More For the Guys, pages 42–43.)

Sizzix or other die cutting and embossing machine
For creating your own die-cut shapes and, with an embossing converter, your own embossed motifs. There are many different sized and shaped die cutters, including alphabets, which are great for adding messages and names to your cards. There is also a wide selection of embossed designs to choose from. (See More Festive Treats, pages 86–87 and More Caring Thoughts, pages 94–95.)

The **side kick** is a die cutting and embossing machine from the Sizzix family. It fits in the palm of your hand and is totally portable. Clamp it to your work surface with the vacuum handle, sandwich your chosen Sizzlits slim die and card between the cutting pads and feed it into the machine. Turn the handle until the cutting plates have passed through and the die-cut shapes come out.

Quick & Clever

Store away any unused and spare die-cut shapes. These can later be mixed and matched or layered up to create quick, unique and impressive embellishments.

Paddle punch

You are not restricted in any way as to where on your card you want to punch with this great tool. There are many different designs, from flowers to butterflies, snowmen to Christmas trees. (See Wedding Elegance, page 56.)

Quick & Clever

If a shape seems stuck in a paddle punch, don't use your fingers to remove it – the dies are very sharp. Simply tap it on the special ejector tool and out it pops.

Round-nosed pliers and wire cutters

Wire cutters will save your best scissors from being ruined and the round-nosed pliers make creating coils and shapes much easier. (See More Festive Treats, pages 86–87.)

Decorative scissors

There are many different styles on the market, but my favourites have to be deckle-edged scissors. You do not need to line up the patterns and the corners do not require any special attention. (See More Loving Wishes, pages 54–55.)

Adhesives

Having the correct glue to hand will allow you to make cards at short notice. As one of the questions I frequently get asked is, 'What glue should I use to stick…?', I've listed the adhesives you will use most often, with tips on how they should be used.

It is very important to use the right adhesive for the right job. For example, I never use wet glue to stick card to card or paper to card, as the moisture can cause the materials to buckle and bend. Follow the advice below and you are sure to achieve great results.

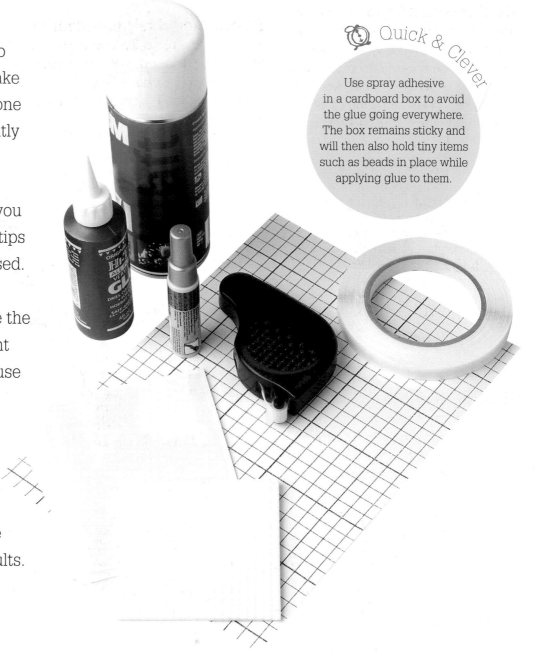

Quick & Clever

Use spray adhesive in a cardboard box to avoid the glue going everywhere. The box remains sticky and will then also hold tiny items such as beads in place while applying glue to them.

Spray adhesive Glue in a spray can. Excellent for sticking fine, handmade papers and serviettes to card. Always read the instructions on the can, and use in a well-ventilated room, or outside. Items can be repositioned carefully.

Glue dots Perfect for sticking fiddly shapes to card. A sheet is made up of tiny dots of glue. Place your item over the glue dots and firm down. The dots of glue will stick to the item.

All-purpose sticky craft glue A tacky craft glue that is used for many different craft applications; from wood to metal, fabric to card and paper. It is a very thick white glue that dries clear, so it is ideal for adding fiddly embellishments such as charms, flat-back crystals or wire to cards.

Double-sided adhesive paper Punch out shapes or use as a backing for a cut-away panel then add foil, glitter or beads to them.

Tape dispensers Simply wipe the cartridge over the back of the item you want to stick down and double-sided tape is applied to it. Dispensers are available in both repositionable and permanent finishes.

Adhesive foam pads These pads are adhesive on both sides – simply remove the backing paper and stick to the card or item. They come in different sizes and are great for achieving a raised effect.

Double-sided tape Comes in a variety of widths; I like to use a narrow one about 5mm (¼in) wide. Always make sure you firm the double-sided tape down well, rub your nail over it to make sure it is well stuck, then it will be easier to remove the backing paper.

Glue pen Ideal for attaching small items as the pens have fine nibs. The glue comes out blue but dries clear – which is great as you can see where it is on the card until it disappears.

Foil writing and images

Use a glue pen to create foil images or writing. Draw or write using the glue pen and leave to dry – it will become clearer. It needs to be very dry, so you could draw one day and add the foil the next. Place the specialist craft foil over the top of the glue, pretty side up. Rub with your fingers to ensure that it has stuck, now carefully lift off the foil.

Positioning design elements

It can be tricky to position some elements correctly on a card, and I have spoilt many cards with a lopsided finish! However, I was shown this technique for using double-sided tape by a print finisher – it allows you to move the element around and reposition it until you have it perfectly placed, then stick it down.

1 Attach double-sided tape to the edges of the element to be stuck to the main card. Then pull back just enough backing paper so that you can see the paper tabs from the front of the card.

2 Position the element on your card, moving it around until you are completely happy with the position. (If all the backing paper is removed you only get one go at positioning.) Firm down where the tape is exposed.

3 Carefully hold the element in the centre and pull the paper tabs off completely. Firm down on the card.

Xyron machine Excellent for applying adhesive to the back of artwork – whatever the shape, this only applies glue where there is somewhere for it to stick. Turn the handle and out comes your self-adhesive artwork, then use the guillotine on the back of the machine to cut it off. Firm down around the edge of the item under the film using your nail to ensure that the glue goes to the edge but no excess glue can escape. Finally, remove the covering film, peel off the backing paper, and the self-adhesive artwork is ready to use. Xyron machines are available in different sizes from 2.5cm (1in) wide to A4 (US letter). You can change the Xyron cartridge to apply magnets or to laminate your work. There is also a small Xyron that is fantastic for small items such as punched-out shapes.

Paper and Card

My love of card making stems from my love of card and paper. There are so many different types to choose from – metallic and pearlized card are my personal favourites, and any shade of purple really catches my eye. This section will help you to choose and store paper and card, allowing you to have to hand the right materials whenever you need to make those last minute greetings cards.

Selecting paper and card

Bear in mind the themes of the cards you most like making, then take into account theme, texture and finish to ensure you buy the most appropriate for your store.

Themes When selecting paper and card, consider who the card is for. Female cards suggest lilac, pinks and soft pastels, while male colours are earthy, such as coppers, greens and blues. Make sure you have good stocks of white, cream and ivory cards: some smooth card for stamping, others with textures and different finishes such as pearlized or metallic. These are a good starting point and you can always add more colours.

Textures Choose from paper and card with an embossed texture such as hammer, linen, watercolour effect, ridged and even leather effect. Other textures include suede, velvet and flock paper, great for adding dimension (see St Patrick's Day, page 104). Most of these can be punched or run through a Sizzix machine to create instant shapes for your cards.

Finishes If you choose a plain card rather than one with a special finish such as a pearlized card, you may have to work slightly harder on the design. An ornate card will only need a simple design to make it truly stunning.

masculine colours

feminine colours

white, cream and ivory paper and card stock

textured paper and card

plain and simple card

pearlized card

Storing paper and card

Here are some top tips to keep your paper and card in perfect condition and easily accessible.

• Store patterned papers in a folder that has been divided up into colour sections (pinks together, blues together and so on). This saves time and keeps the paper flat and in pristine condition.

• Store scored and folded cards firstly by size, then shape, colour, texture, aperture and so on. You will usually know what size card you want to make, so you will know where to start looking.

• Keep a supply of A4 (US letter) card in various colours so you can score and fold your own cards. This is useful for making cards in unusual sizes or shapes.

A good storage system is essential for finding the paper and card you need, when you need it.

Other features

Look out for card and paper that will make your greetings all the more special – storing a range of materials such as these will give you more creative options and flexibility.

Patterned There is a fabulous range of patterned background papers on the market in every colour and pattern imaginable.

Apertures Blank cards with apertures are widely available, and the apertures come in all shapes and sizes.

Shaped Choose from handbags to butterflies, teapots to watering cans and even cars for cards with a real difference, no matter what the special occasion.

Embossed Wonderful for beginners as the embossed design will guide you in placing the embellishments.

Paper vellum Available in a variety of colours, patterns and finishes, including embossed varieties.

Specialist For something different, choose from some of the specialist cards on offer such as glittered cards, watercolour cards with glitter shapes or thick Plasma plastic cards.

Paper Techniques

With a few very simple skills you can work with paper and card to create different looks and styles for your greetings cards in next to no time. Try making unique patterned papers, creating torn edges or experimenting with different ways of layering paper vellum on to card.

Scoring and folding your own cards

If you wish to fold your own cards use one of these simple techniques for achieving a crisp, clean, professional finish.

Scoring

Measure and mark on the card where you wish to make the fold. Place in a paper trimmer, lining the mark up with the groove that cuts the card. Starting at the top, pull an embossing tool down the groove to score the card. Alternatively, use a ruler with a bone folder held in an upright position.

Folding

Align the edges of the card and use a bone folder held flat to flatten the crease carefully.

Quick & Clever

This scoring and folding board makes creating perfectly creased cards easy. Cut the card to size then line up one edge with the raised edge on the board. Find the groove for the card size you are making and score the card by dragging an embossing tool down the groove. Turn the card over and place one edge against the raised edge of the board and fold the card so the two edges align perfectly.

Paper sizes

Below is a useful outline of the different card sizes most frequently used in card making. The most common size is A5 – two A5 cards can be cut and folded from one sheet of A4 (US letter). In the card trade A5 is often referred to as C6, which is the size of envelopes used for the folded A5 card.

Rectangular Card

name of card	size of card
A4 (US letter)	21 × 29.5cm (8¼ × 11⅝in)
A5 or C6 (half A4)	14.8 × 21cm (5¾ × 8¼in)
A6 (half A5)	10.5 × 14.8cm (4⅛ × 5¾in)

Square Card

I use two standard size square cards 12cm (4¾in) and 15cm (6in). Both of them can be cut from a single sheet of A4 (US letter). They are also standard sizes for shop-bought blanks.

name of card	made from
12cm (4¾in) square	24 × 12cm (9½ × 4¾in) scored and folded
15cm (6in) square	30 × 15cm (12 × 6in) scored and folded

Sourcing paper

Buy at least two sheets of card or paper at a time, so that you always have one spare sheet. Keep this sheet to store (see page 17), writing in pencil on the back the details of where you bought it. If you need more of the same type you will be able to source it again.

Creating patterned backgrounds

When you can't find exactly the right patterned paper, or you can't get to the shops, here are a couple of simple techniques for making your own patterned papers using materials you are likely to have in your craft box as stencils.

Punches

Punch a design out of a piece of scrap card. Now take an inkpad and sponge and apply colour to the card through the aperture. Move it around the card, going on and off the card to create a stunning background.

Peel-off stickers

Place a peel-off sticker on the card then sponge on ink to add colour just over the edges. Sponge gently and add soft touches of colour: you can add ink but you can't take it away. Lift and move the sticker around the card, adding colour and going over the edges of the paper.

Use peel-off stickers to create an interesting background design.

Tearing paper

Tearing paper gives a very natural, handmade effect to your cards. It softens lines and creates a natural feel.

Paper and paper vellum

Always tear the paper towards you to open up the layers. If the paper or card is coloured on one side and white on the other you will create a white torn edge. Paper vellum can be torn in the same way, and whatever the colour, you will always get a white edge showing.

Mulberry paper

To give a wispy edge to this delicate paper, wet the edges and gently tease it apart. (See Teddy is Tops, page 102.)

Quick & Clever

Use a spray adhesive when sticking mulberry paper to card as the paper is translucent and tape and glue will show through.

Attaching paper vellum to cards

Because it is translucent, paper vellum is tricky to attach to cards without the glue showing. Try these techniques to overcome this.

Double-sided tape

Use very small pieces of tape to attach paper vellum to card, then cover up with peel-off stickers.

Vellum glue pen

Apply to the paper vellum then stick down – the glue does not show. It needs to dry thoroughly so the glue sticks.

Brads

Cut a slit in the paper vellum and card (cut through both layers together) push the brad through, turn the card over and open out the legs.

Hole punch and ribbon

Punch two holes through both the card and vellum, positioning them centrally, then thread the ribbon through the holes to attach it to the card.

Peel-off stickers

Cut the paper vellum slightly smaller than the card it is to be attached to. Position stickers half over the vellum and half on the card to secure.

Embellishments

After the paper and card, the main ingredient for an eye-catching finish is the embellishment. The choice available is simply staggering, and growing all the time. Here are some great choices for making instant cards, with some useful hints, tips and techniques for using them.

Peel-off stickers

An incredibly quick and versatile embellishment. There are thousands to choose from, from contemporary floral and butterfly designs to useful eyelets and text messages.

Using the waste

Use frosted tape to lift up the bits of sticker that are left behind when you have used the outline. (This technique only works for designs that still have part of the outline to complete the picture.) Firm frosted tape over the design then lift away, ensuring all the little bits have stuck to the tape. Place on card and rub the back of the tape so that all the bits stick to the card. Carefully remove the tape, leaving the waste stuck to your card.

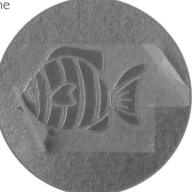

Stickers

There are stunning stickers around that look fantastic on cards. Most are self adhesive, so you simply peel them from their backing paper and stick them to your cards. You can change their appearance by mounting them on to coloured card or embellish them with flat-backed crystals, glitter glue, beads, ribbons, threads and much more. (See Halloween Magic, page 80.)

Quick & Clever

Remove and transfer peel-off stickers with a craft knife. Never hold them in two hands, as they stretch out of shape, especially peel-off lettering stickers.

Storing embellishments

Be organized – keep separate boxes for stickers, brads, buttons, eyelets, ribbon, thread and other items. Sort brads by design and colour so that you know where to look for a particular type. This saves so much time as you can easily lay your hand on just the embellishment you need.

Brads

There are many different brad designs and sizes available – circles, squares, hearts, flowers, shiny and matt or crystal and pearl – to create features in your design, for attaching vellum or mounting card to card. (See A Birthday Catch, page 40.)

Fixing a brad

1 Use a craft knife to cut a small slit in your card. Push the legs of the brad through the hole in the card.

2 Turn the card over and open out the legs of the brad on the back of the card, pressing them flat.

Eyelets

Eyelets come in a variety of shapes and sizes: circles, hearts, flowers, squares and even planes, boats and trains! You will need an eyelet punch, setter tool and hammer and a cutting mat to work on. Eyelets make great decorations or can be used to attach vellum or other coloured card and motifs to your card.

Fixing an eyelet

1 Working on a cutting mat, use the punch to create a hole in your card for the eyelet.

2 Place the eyelet upside down, then turn the card wrong side up and line up the hole with the eyelet, use the setter tool and the hammer to set the eyelet in your card.

> ⏰ *Quick & Clever*
>
> Circle eyelets make effective flower centres and car wheels. Try using the very tiny circle eyelets as the buttons on a rubber stamped shirt.

Punches

Some amazing cards can be made using punches, and many different shapes and sizes are available. Border punches add fancy edges to your work (1), plier punches (2) in different shapes create smaller designs on your cards, and a vast range of motif punches (3) create embellishments. The paddle punch allows you to punch anywhere on your card (see Wedding Elegance, page 56). You can also use punches to create stencil designs (see page 19).

> ⏰ *Quick & Clever*
>
> To use a punch, simply place the paper or card into the punch, push down on the design, and out pops your instant shape. You can use the negative space left behind or the punched motif.

Rubber stamping

Rubber stamps produce an instant image that you can colour and embellish any way you please. There are different types of equipment associated with rubber stamping, and having the right accessories will allow you to create cards much faster.

The basic technique

- Work on a firm flat surface – a cutting mat is ideal. Place copy paper on the cutting mat to save marking it with inks.
- Ink the stamp evenly to cover all of the design. Take the inkpad to the stamp for more control over the amount of ink used.
- Tap gently all over – check the stamp before stamping.
- Use both hands to hold the stamp if necessary, and never let go completely while stamping.
- With larger stamps, hold the stamp with one hand and use the other hand to push gently and evenly all over the picture area.
- Hold the card or paper you are stamping on with one hand and lift the stamp off with the other.

Equipment

Unmounted and clear stamps (1) are used with clear acrylic blocks, perfect for placing your design accurately as you can see where you are stamping. They don't need much storage space.

Wood mounted stamps (2) often come with pre-coloured decals, making it easier to copy and achieve similar results with repeat patterns.

A craft heat tool (3) is used to heat and melt embossing powder.

Black permanent ink (4) is great for watercolours as, once dry, it won't run.

Pearlescent ink (5) can be embossed, but also gives excellent results on its own. It dries quickly on matt card.

An embossing inkpad (6) is used with embossing powder or to give a watermark effect – it turns matt card a shade darker, ideal for backgrounds.

Gold or silver embossing powder (7) sprinkled on to a stamped image and heated gives a raised and shiny finish.

An antistatic bag (8) wiped over card before embossing ensures the powder only sticks to the stamped image and doesn't mark the card.

Stamp care

Cleaning stamps Always clean stamps after use. Use a rubber stamp cleaner or add water to a stamp cleaner pad with bristles: drag your stamp one way to clean all the ink off. Dry stamps before putting them away or near inkpads.

Storage Always store stamps rubber side down – making it easier to find the one you want – and away from direct sunlight. You can put one stamp on top of another but do not throw them in as they can get damaged.

Quick & Clever

To add instant glamour, experiment with the many different types of embossing powders – from gold, silver and copper through to specialist pearl, crystal and glitter ones.

Embossing

When embossing, use a pigment or embossing inkpad – this is special ink that stays wet long enough to sprinkle the embossing powder over. Tap the excess off and use the heat tool to melt the powder, leaving a raised, shiny image. Don't touch the embossing until it has cooled. You can also colour in this design, or use eyecatching metallic card alone.

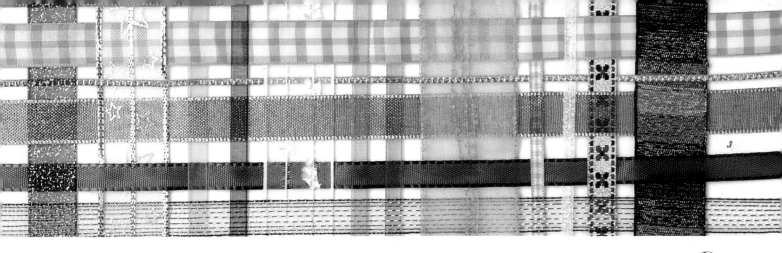

Decorative details

These are the pretty embellishments that add that extra special touch to your cards. They are fun to collect and fabulous to use.

Ribbons There are so many different styles and sizes of ribbon to choose from: plain, sheer, patterned, thin, wide.
Instant effects Try stamping pictures or messages on to ribbon using a permanent inkpad, or colouring them with different inks such as pearlized or multi-dye pads. Stamping a message on the card then masking with a sheer ribbon adds an air of mystery!

Threads Metallic, embroidery or frayed thread along with twine and string all add interesting touches.
Instant effects Use a square corner cutter then wrap thread around the edges of your card. For added embellishment, glue crystals to them. Add to tags and buttons for the perfect finishing touch.

Wire This comes in a wonderful wide range of colours and different thicknesses (gauges). The higher the number the thinner the wire: 22 gauge bends easily and holds it shape well – you can even create words with it.

Buttons Available in gorgeous colours and in many sizes and shapes. Buttons add a funky or whimsical feel depending on the colour you choose.

Crystals These come in an almost infinite variety of colours, sizes and shapes and they add amazing sparkle to your cards.
Instant application Crystals can be fiddly, so a hot-fix wand used with special hot-fix crystals is a useful tool. With different sized heads and variable temperatures, it sticks the crystals to the card. Alternatively, attach normal crystals with a tiny dab of all-purpose sticky craft glue applied with a kebab stick or positioning tool (see page 48).

Beads Choose from long bugle beads, tiny seed beads or plain beads in a vast range of colours and finishes. They are another great way to add sparkle to your card.

Confetti There is a massive range of confetti to match every occasion available from card and craft stores.
Instant effects Stick on confetti as embellishments, or add a pinch of confetti to the inside of the card or envelope so it falls out when the card is opened.

Choosing Colour

The colour of your card is one of the most important elements in the design; it can make or break the finished look. However, you must also remember that much of card making is what appeals to you: if you like it, that's all that really matters. Being familiar with how colours work together and the effects achieved will make choosing colours for new cards much easier – especially if you need a card in a hurry!

The colour wheel

A colour wheel makes choosing colours that work together really easy. It shows the primary, secondary and tertiary colours. Primary colours are red, blue and yellow. Secondary colours are the result of mixing two of the three primary colours together: green from blue and yellow; orange from red and yellow; and purple from red and blue. When you start to mix the primary colours with the secondary colours you get tertiary colours such as aqua, puce and lime.

Make an impact

For instant impact, choose colours that are opposite one another on the wheel – red and green, blue and orange, and purple and yellow. These are called complementary colours and work together to give bold and vibrant results. A softer effect requires a combination of colours that are next to each other on the wheel, known as analogous colours.

Red and green are complementary colours so lime green, orange and purple make a striking combination.

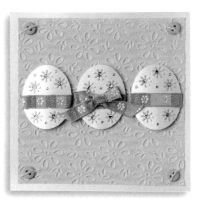

Lime green, yellow and warm yellow sit next to each other on the colour wheel, creating a harmonious whole.

Temperature control

The choice of cool or warm colours has an immediate effect on a card design. The colours on the wheel, from red, clockwise round to green, are known as warm colours. Aqua round to puce are cool colours. Match gold or copper with warm colours and silver tones with cool colours.

warm

cool

Quick & Clever

If a sheet of card or an embellishment catches your eye, try to buy other elements such as brads and inkpads in matching colours at the same time to ensure you always have coordinating materials.

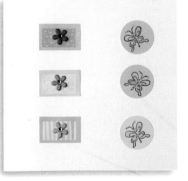

Colourful occasions

When designing a card for a specific occasion, certain colours spring to mind that will create an instant message or mood.

Earthy

Warm colours such as red and green in earthy tones combine well for natural themes (see page 40).

Pastel

Pale hues of any colour create soft pastels that mix well together for a pretty result (see page 46).

Gold, yellow and cream for a golden wedding anniversary.

Lilac, pink, coral, blues or greens reflect the delicate hues of spring.

Elegant

Cool colours give an elegant finish to this stylish stamped design (see page 48).

Rich

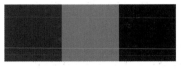

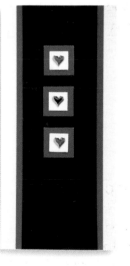

Warm, rich reds combine with antique gold for a tasteful look (see page 52).

Copper, gold, deep green and rich reds create an autumnal or festive feel.

Citrus yellow, limes and oranges remind us of summer.

Design and Layout

Becoming familiar with how design layouts work will allow you to become more confident, and to create your own designs far more quickly. The first thing to think about when making a card is who it is for and what you want to use. Then you can begin work on the layout.

Experiment with the different elements until you have a layout and design that you like. A set square will help you position the elements correctly and quickly – use the markings on the set square to measure the gaps between each element accurately (see Equipment, page 11). Good spacing will give your cards a professional look. When you are happy with the positioning, stick your embellishments down.

Design tips

Here are six different layouts for cards using the same elements: an oblong and three or four little accents. Each one looks balanced, and therefore is pleasing to the eye because the following design principles were applied:

• Borders around the edges of elements are equal for a professional, balanced finish.
• Accents are placed carefully to provide harmonious visual balance for the main design element.
• When a strong design statement is required, elements are placed deliberately off centre.
• For a simple but bold effect and immediate focus, elements are positioned in the centre.

Quick & Clever

Experiment with different elements and layouts to help you understand design principles, decide what works for you, and so design cards quickly.

Creating a theme

When designing your card it is important to take into account the whole package: the front, inside with message, back (signed and dated so that the recipient knows it is handmade) and the envelope too. If you carry the theme all the way through it gives a professional finish.

The card has a tag with punched out daisies on it, with smaller daisies in the bottom right corner which continue the theme and balance the design.

On the back of the card include the same daisy along with your signature and the date you made the card.

Inside the card two more daisies continue the theme and there is room for a message. You can rubber stamp the message, use peel-off stickers, hand write it or print it from your computer.

To complete the theme, part of the envelope has been masked with a piece of scrap paper, and then the exposed area sponged using an inkpad that matched the card. Once dry, three punched out daisies were added.

Making inserts

Add an insert to the card for a truly professional and luxurious feel. It's also a quick way to hide elements that show through on the inside, such as eyelets or brads.

Colour and texture Choose paper to complement the card and the occasion. Pick a colour either to match your card, or to achieve a subtle or bold contrast. Parchment-effect paper with a faint pattern gives a fantastic finish, and comes in many different colours. You can print on to paper vellum, which is available in many different colours.

Embellishment Cut with fancy-edged scissors, or apply a gold, silver or coloured pen to the edge, linking it to the card's main colour theme. Try to keep decorations subtle.

Attaching the insert To attach a paper vellum insert, punch two holes in the centre of the card and thread ribbon through to secure (see right).

To attach the insert with double-sided tape, first cut the insert paper 6mm (¼in) smaller than the card all the way round then fold in half and crease using a bone folder. Apply double-sided tape to the back of the folded insert then place into the folded card. Open the card from the back so that you can see the double-sided tape and remove the backing paper (see right). Shut the card, firming down along the crease of the card

Attaching the insert using ribbon

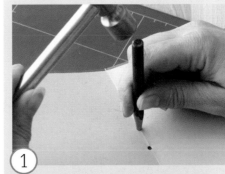

① Layer the folded insert and card together and punch two holes in the centre folds.

② Thread the ribbon through and tie a bow on the front of the card.

Producing Cards in Bulk

Some occasions call for several cards of the same design, and you can save yourself a lot of money by making your own. It is great to personalize cards for a special birthday, wedding anniversary or even a themed party. You may also need bulk cards to announce the birth of a new baby, a christening, a wedding, a new home and, of course, at Christmas.

Creating the design

When producing cards in bulk you need to make sure your design is simple so it can be produced quickly. Pick your colours. Do you want to be traditional or contemporary? Do you want to stamp the cards or use the Sizzix die cutter, emboss them or use stickers? If you plan well and follow a few simple rules you will soon be posting your cards – whether it's 10 or 100 you need to make!

Quick & Clever

When ordering your cards and envelopes, order some spares in case of mishaps. Doing this in advance saves time, money and ensures the company haven't run out of your chosen card just when you need more!

Embellish a ready-made card blank with a simple design for a quick batch of Christmas cards (see More Winter Wishes, page 90).

A card with simple design elements will be quicker to make for bulk wedding invitations (see More Romance, page 58).

Card stock for multiples

Prepare ahead and save time without compromising the finish.
• To cut, score and fold your own cards would take several days, so pre-scored and folded cards are ideal for multiple makes – a professional look in an instant.
• Consider the theme and choose colours to match (see page 24). Pearlized card will add instant interest; mirrored card provides in-built shine. Select the right colour and finish and your design work is half done.
• Save time by ordering good quality envelopes that will make your cards extra special – gold and silver foil envelopes add immediate luxury.
• Pre-embossed cards provide a basic layout and an easy guide to placing the elements. This ensures that every card is made with ease and precision.

The amazing variety of card blanks available today makes producing handmade cards in large quantities easier than ever before.

Finishing touches

Printing messages on to inserts on the computer is ideal for ensuring the cards say just what you want (see page 27 for making inserts). Pick a font (text style) that matches the occasion, and paper that tones with the card.

Don't forget to decorate the envelopes, perhaps with just a small version of the design – this adds the finishing touch and co-ordinates the package (see pages 27–29). Allow yourself plenty of time for the project; cards made with care and attention will look far nicer than those rushed at the last minute.

Production lines

Enlist the help of family and friends as this will help to spread the load and get the job done much more quickly. It's also fun working together.
• Create a clear working area and set up a table for the production line.
• Keep the working area tidy and organized.
• Prepare in advance: punch out shapes, stamp backgrounds, sort embellishments.
• Allocate a job for each person in assembling the card.

Quick & Clever

To keep production time to a minimum, ensure your materials are organized. For example, store crystals in a pillbox – it has compartments to store crystals by size and colour, making it easy to find what is required instantly.

Making for occasions

Special occasions often call for multiple cards – here are some examples of projects featured in this book that are ideal to make in bulk. Remember, you can always adapt the original design to suit your specific purpose.

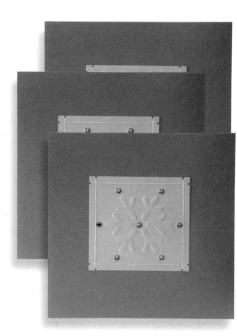

Making your own Christmas cards can save money, and with a simple but effective design it doesn't have to be time-consuming. Gather your materials in advance and leave plenty of time for assembly. (See Season's Greetings, page 88 and Instant Celebrations, Yuletide Greetings page 99.)

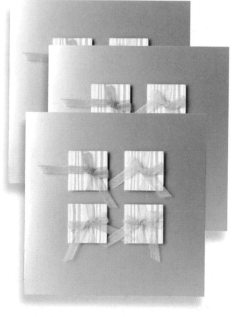

Preparing for a party is such fun, and making your own invitations to reflect the occasion, such as a child's first birthday, can really add to the excitement. (See Pretty Prezzies, page 47, Birthday Bonanza, page 102 and St Patrick's Day, page 104.)

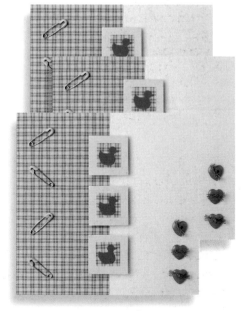

With the arrival of a new baby, there isn't always a lot of time for making announcement cards. However, with a bit of planning and a simple design, a personalized card is easy to produce in bulk in the run up to the big day. (See The Pitter Patter, page 68, and More Bundles of Joy, page 74.)

Selling Your Cards

Once you have perfected your technique for making instant cards, you may find that your production even begins to outstrip your needs! This would be a good time to consider selling the extras. You may not make a fortune but you will, at least, cover your costs.

Where to start

There are many different ways to sell your handmade cards. You can, of course, sell to friends and family and this is how most people get started. If you work in an office, this is another invaluable source of custom. In this case, a good way to display your cards for sale is in a photo album where the cards won't get touched or damaged.

Many people find it convenient to buy cards from outlets they regularly visit such as local gift shops, florists, coffee shops and even hairdressers. Many big department stores buy direct from crafters so don't be afraid to approach them. Send them a professional-looking card sample and a covering letter. Card shops tend to buy in bulk so you are more likely to be successful approaching smaller outlets.

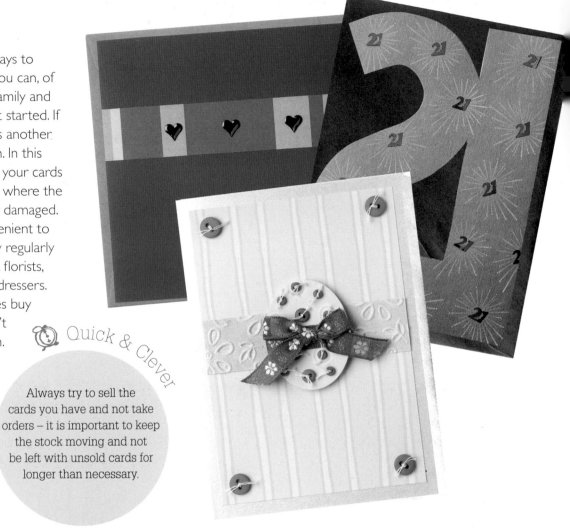

Quick & Clever

Always try to sell the cards you have and not take orders – it is important to keep the stock moving and not be left with unsold cards for longer than necessary.

Selling to shops

There are two main ways of doing business with shops.
• Firstly, there is sale or return, which is what the shop is most likely to want. Take a selection of cards into them and agree what you are willing to pay the shop for selling them – usually a percentage of the cost of each card. Leave them for an allotted time, then return to see what has sold and collect your money – paying the shop their fee – and take back the unsold cards. Keep a list of the cards you leave there, and check off what has been sold so that you know what to make again.
• The other way is to take a number of cards into the shop and sell them to the shopkeeper for a set price per card, or for ten or twenty cards. The shop then sells them for whatever they feel they can charge. I prefer to work like this, as you receive the money as you make the cards – and then you can start again.

You probably make slightly more money working on sale and return. However the unsold cards may have been damaged and, of course, you still have to sell them.

Top tips for cards that sell

Size C6 is the most common size card and this is the standard card rack size. If you are buying blanks, this will keep the cost down as every card supplier stocks C6 and many will offer special deals.

Matching envelopes give a professional look

Use the most common card sizes to fit racks.

Position design elements towards the top of the card for maximum impact on the shelves.

Quality Buy the best card stock you can afford, as cheap card stock will make cheap looking cards. Invest in a matching envelope – if you use more expensive looking foil, gold or silver envelopes you will find that you can charge more for your cards.

Design Position the main design elements towards the top of the card – the part visible on the rack. Offer a selection for all occasions – birthdays are most popular – and remember to cater for all ages and both sexes.

Pricing Price your cards individually. Don't under price your cards – ensure you cover the cost of the materials used, plus some profit. You may not cover your time, but you can enjoy the fruits of a hobby you really love.

Quick & Clever

Always pack your cards in polypropylene bags: they are inexpensive and help to protect the cards and keep them clean. They also provide a professional presentation.

Marketing

Labels printed with your contact details are ideal for the card bags, so customers know how to get hold of more of your cards. Stamp the back of your cards to show customers they are handmade and by whom. Have a rubber stamp made with a little motif and your name, and include your telephone number (the recipient of the card won't have the bag featuring your details).

Card Design by Your Name
tel: 01234 567890
email and website addresses

Let's Go!

Birthday Charm

For girlfriends who love to shop, these fun gold charms are a quick way to make an eye-catching birthday card. Buy a folded plastic card – it is difficult to fold by hand – and embellish to create a vibrant, modern look. For a man, choose deeper or more earthy colours and add gardening or sports charms.

You will need

- 15cm (6in) folded square pink plasma card
- 2 sheets of frames and labels in pink, red and orange
- Pink, red and orange striped paper
- 5 flower-shaped brads in pink and orange
- Flat-back crystals in pink and orange
- Purple sheer ribbon
- Shoe and handbag charms
- 1 pink plastic flower

1

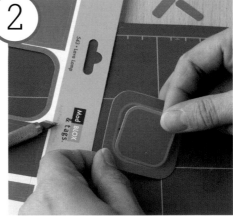

Cut an 8 × 15cm (3⅛ × 6in) panel of striped paper. Use a craft knife to make small slits in all four corners of the paper, push the flower brads through and bend back the legs to secure. Stick the striped panel to the left front of the card using double-sided tape. Stick a matching orange or pink flat-back crystal in the centre of each flower brad using all-purpose sticky craft glue and leave to dry.

Quick & Clever

Decorate the inside using striped paper and a tag, and add flower brads. Punch six daisies from orange paper. Glue these to the inside and back of the card to cover the back of the brads.

2

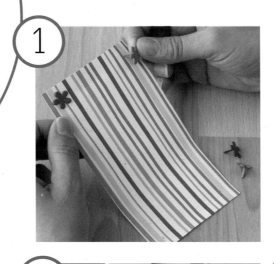

Select a frame and three small labels from the sheet. The labels and frames are 'kiss' cut – they are cut out but caught in a few places to hold them in place. Use a craft knife to cut through the little tabs neatly. Use adhesive foam pads to stick the frame in the top half of the patterned paper and double-sided tape to stick the three labels on the bottom right side of the plastic card.

3

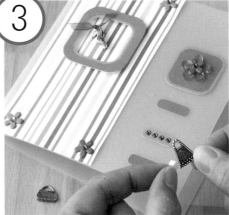

Tie the ribbon to the shoe charm and stick inside the frame using an adhesive foam pad. Put a flower brad in the centre hole of the plastic flower, then cut a small slit in the square label, push the brad through and open the legs. Stick this above the small labels using double-sided tape and glue a flat-back crystal to the centre of the flower. Add the handbag charms using adhesive foam pads and glue four pink flat-back crystals to the orange label using all-purpose sticky craft glue.

More for the girls

Sheets of frames, circles and blocks in fresh, fruity citrus colours are the basis of these clever cards. As well as being great for birthdays, they work equally well as a rejuvenating get-well message or special thank you.

Say it with Flowers

You will need

- 15cm (6in) folded square gold card
- Frames in citrus colours
- 3 flower rubber stamps
- Permanent black inkpad
- Watercolour pencils or felt tip pens
- Glitter glue

be inspired by . . .

brads

buttons

floral rubber stamps

flat-back crystals

bright paper shapes

Cut three narrow frames from your sheet leaving the centre panels in place. Stamp a different flower in the centre panel of each. Leave to dry. Colour the flowers in with either watercolour pencils or felt tip pens. Evenly space them across the top half of the card and stick in place with adhesive foam pads. Apply highlights of glitter glue to the flower heads and leave to dry.

It's your special day

Let's party

Happy birthday

If friends were flowers I'd pick you

May your birthday be as special as you are

Lazy Daisy

Cut out the block with a craft knife. Cut a small slit in the centre. Push the flower brad through the centre hole in the plastic flower, then through the slit and open the legs to secure. Stick the block in the centre front of the card with double-sided tape. Cut out a circle tag and add a sticker eyelet. Wrap the ribbon around the front of the card near the fold, thread the circle tag on to the ribbon and tie a double knot, trim the ends. Stick a flat-back crystal in the centre of the circle tag flower and to the flower brad using all-purpose sticky craft glue. Leave to dry.

You will need

- 12cm (4¾in) folded square green card
- Blocks and circles in citrus colours
- Green plastic flower
- Green flower shaped brad
- Lime sheer ribbon
- Green flat-back crystals
- Black peel-off sticker eyelet

You will need

- 15cm (6in) folded square gold card
- Frames and circles in mixed colours
- Flower shaped brads in pink, orange and green
- Flat-back crystals in pink, orange and green
- Butterfly rubber stamp
- Permanent black inkpad
- Glitter glue

Spring Greetings

Using a craft knife cut out three centre tags from the frames sheet. Cut a small slit in the centre of each one and insert a flower brad, opening the legs to secure. Space the tags evenly down the left side of the card and stick with double-sided tape. Stick a flat-back crystal to the centre of each flower brad using all-purpose sticky craft glue and leave to dry. Rubber stamp a butterfly in the centre of three circles and leave to dry. Position the circles alongside the tags on the right of the card and secure with double-sided tape. Highlight the butterflies with glitter glue.

A Birthday Catch

An angler's dream: this greetings card makes use of embossed card and paper vellum both with a fishy theme. Keep an eye out for materials that reflect the interests of your nearest and dearest men and adapt this design to make a unique card that will be truly treasured by the recipient.

You will need

- 15cm (6in) folded square copper card
- Extra copper card
- Hole and square punch
- Fish embossed paper vellum
- Fish embossed card
- Brads
- Fishing hooks
- Household string

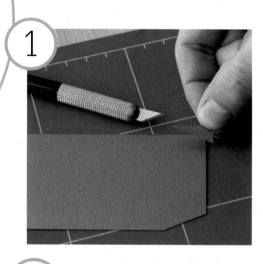

1 Cut a 5 x 11cm (2 x 4⅜in) panel from the copper card to make a tag. Snip one corner from the tag then place this piece over the opposite corner and mark with a craft knife before cutting – this ensures both corners are the same. Punch a hole in the top of the tag.

Quick & Clever

If you have silver wire in your toolbox you could bend and shape small lengths to make your own fish hooks. Use round-nosed pliers for the job.

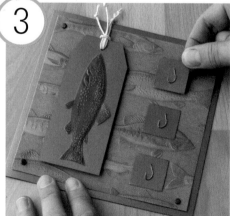

2 Carefully cut out one of the fish designs from the paper vellum and mount on the copper tag using a glue pen. Cut a square of embossed card slightly smaller than the folded copper card, so that it leaves a narrow border all the way round. Make a small slit at each corner of the embossed fish card and put the legs of the brads through from the front. Stick to the card using double-sided tape.

3 Open out the legs. Punch three squares from the copper card and stick a fishing hook to each one with all-purpose sticky craft glue. Leave to dry. Add string to the tag and stick the tag to the front left of the card with adhesive foam pads. Use double-sided tape to stick the three squares with the hooks down the right-hand side.

More cool kids

Pastel-coloured paper, ribbons, beads and silver card give a lovely soft look to these fun children's cards. Balloons, presents and candles are perfect for birthday greetings or party invitations, and using bright primary colours instead would make them perfect for boys as well.

Up, Up and Away

sheer ribbon

balloon punch

bugle beads

striped paper and silver card

You will need

- 15cm (6in) folded square silver card
- Lilac, yellow, green and pink pastel card
- Square and balloon punch
- Striped paper
- Silver wire

Punch out four squares, one each from lilac, yellow, green and pink pastel card. Stick to the front of the card with double-sided tape. Punch four balloons from the striped paper. Bend and shape some silver wire to make the strings and wrap around the bottom of the balloons. Using adhesive foam pads, stick a balloon on each of the punched squares.

Come to my party

Let's party

For a special son/daughter

It's your day to shine

It's your special day: enjoy!

Pretty Prezzies

Punch out four squares from the striped paper and stick them to white card using double-sided tape, trim around the edges. Wrap each parcel with a different coloured length of thin sheer ribbon and tie in a bow. Mount the parcels on the front of the silver card using adhesive foam pads.

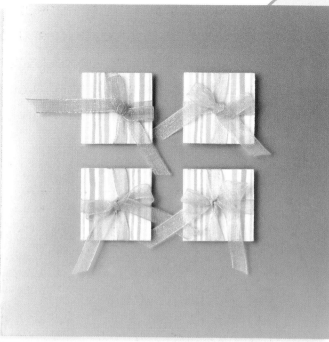

You will need

- 15cm (6in) square folded silver card
- Striped paper
- Square punch
- White card
- Lilac, blue, green and pink pastel thin sheer ribbon

You will need

- 15cm (6in) folded square silver card
- Lilac, blue, yellow and pink pastel card
- Square and mini star punches
- Bugle beads

Four Birthday Wishes

Punch a square out of lilac card and, using all-purpose sticky craft glue, stick bugle beads on the front to make four candles. Using double-sided tape mount the lilac card first on blue card, then yellow and finally pink card. Trim each time to leave a different coloured border all the way round. Punch small stars out of different coloured card and glue to the top of the candles. Stick to the centre-front of the card with double-sided tape.

More special birthdays

Eye-catching birthday confetti set off by celebration starbursts were the inspiration for these coming of age cards. You can easily change the colours to suit a young woman or man or use confetti to mark other significant birthdays if wished. These cards make great party invitations as well.

Shake, Rattle and Roll ✓

21 and 18 confetti

starburst rubber stamp

brightly coloured card

You will need

- A4 (US letter) pink card, halved then scored and folded to make A5
- Blue card mat with two apertures, slightly smaller than A5
- Starburst rubber stamp
- White inkpad
- 21 confetti
- Acetate
- Adhesive foam strip

Stamp a design of white starbursts over the blue card then stick 21s inside the centre of each stamp using a glue pen. Cut a rectangle of acetate slightly larger than the square aperture and secure to the back of the blue card using double-sided tape. Place adhesive foam strips around the aperture to create a cavity then add a handful of confetti. Close the cavity by attaching a second piece of acetate to the foam strips. Stick the blue card matt to the pink card with foam pads in each corner. Stick two pink and one blue 21 in the oblong aperture.

21 today

18 today

Celebrate in style

Enjoy your special day

Hoping your day is special in every way

18 Today

Trace off the 18 template (see page 107), transfer to the front of the card and cut out. Randomly stamp blue starbursts over the 18 shape and stick 18 confetti to the centres using the glue pen. This card is great for boys and girls – simply change the colour of the card.

You will need

- A4 (US letter) blue card, scored and folded to make A5
- Starburst rubber stamp
- Blue inkpad
- 18 confetti

You will need

- A4 (US letter) blackcurrant card, scored and folded to make A5
- Starburst rubber stamp
- White inkpad
- 21 confetti

Star Spangled Celebration

Trace off the 21 template (see page 108), transfer to the blackcurrant card and cut out. Stamp white starbursts randomly over the shaped card and stick a 21 confetti to the centre of each pattern using a glue pen.

ribbon

champagne
rubber
stamp

peel-off sticker
hearts

red, silver
and
bronze
card

More anniversary ideas

The colours of some special anniversaries – silver, ruby and gold – are the basis of these special cards, plus the heart as an emblem of love and champagne glasses to toast the happy couple. Paper vellum is a terrific material and the pocket on 'Sent with Love' would be a great place to display a keepsake picture.

Sent with Love

You will need

- 12cm (4¾in) folded square card in cream
- Clear paper vellum
- Red, silver or gold card
- Hole and scallop-edged heart punch
- String

Trace off the small pocket template (see page 106) straight on to the vellum and cut out. Fold in the three edges using a bone folder and stick to the front of the folded card using double-sided tape. Punch the heart out of red, silver or gold card, punch a hole in the top and thread through a length of string. Pop the heart in the vellum pocket.

You are the love of my life

My heart belongs to you

For two very special people

Together is a wonderful place to be

For the special times we've shared together

Anniversary Toast

You will need

- 15cm (6in) folded square card in cream or silver
- Gold, red or silver paper vellum
- Champagne glasses rubber stamp
- Gold, clear or silver embossing powder
- Gold, red or silver embossing inkpad
- Gold, white or dark silver card
- Bronze, red or silver card for mounting
- Large, medium and small peel-off sticker hearts in gold, red or silver
- Gold, red or silver sheer ribbon

Cut a 9 x 15cm (3⅝ x 6in) panel of paper vellum in your chosen colour then fold in 2cm (¾in) and secure to the back folded edge of the card with a thin strip of double-sided tape. Rubber stamp the champagne glasses on to you chosen card, using the correct coloured embossing powder for the anniversary. Mount the stamped design on to the correct coloured card and stick an adhesive foam pad in each corner. Stretch and hold the vellum down and place the mounted stamped design half on the vellum and half on the card. This will secure the vellum without using any extra glue. Decorate the vellum panel with the appropriate coloured peel-off sticker hearts. Add three small hearts to the bottom right corner of the card then tie a sheer ribbon near the folded edge and secure with a bow.

Keys to the Door

An amazing embossing board with a design etched into it is the key to making this stylish card quickly and easily. Simply place your card over the top and trace off the design with an embossing tool. Add house keys with a number tag to match the house and you have the perfect welcome to a new home.

You will need

- 15cm (6in) square bought blank cream card with printed blue strip
- 7 x 11cm (2¾ x 5⅞in) sapphire blue card for embossing
- Blue pearlized and silver card
- House embossing board and tool
- Square brads
- Key punch
- Black eyelet and numbers peel-off stickers
- Metal tag and ball chain

1

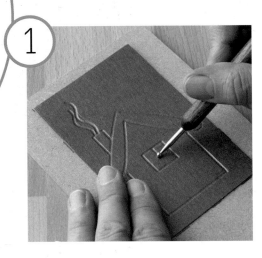

Place the sapphire blue card right side up on the embossing board and, using an embossing tool, trace over the pattern of the house. You may need to lift the card to see where the design begins, but then it is easy to follow.

Quick & Clever

If you use good quality card and the embossing tool slips off the pattern, the marks that show on the back of the card will not show on the front.

Quick & Clever

Adding black eyelet stickers to the keys and tag not only highlights the holes attractively but serves a practical purpose, as the chain might otherwise damage the card.

2

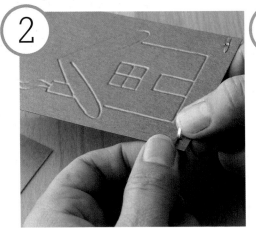

Cut slits in the four corners of the sapphire card and put the legs of the brads through, turn the card over and open them out flat. If the brads go beyond the edge of the card trim them with scissors. Mount on blue card with double-sided tape and trim to leave a small border showing. Stick the image on the centre of the white area of the main card using double-sided tape.

3

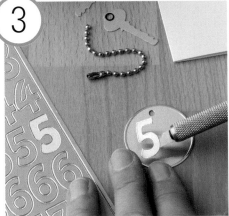

Punch two keys from the silver card and add a peel-off sticker eyelet to each one. Use a craft knife to lift the numbers from the sticker sheet and position on the metal tag; add an eyelet sticker. Thread the keys and metal tag on to the chain then lock the two ends together. Mount the tag and keys on the blue strip using adhesive foam pads.

The Pitter Patter...

What a wonderful way to announce the arrival of twins: a cute stamp creates the effect of printed baby feet – in a fraction of the time and without the mess! I've made this card to welcome a multiple birth, but just one pair of mounted feet on a slightly smaller card is perfect for a single bundle of joy.

You will need

- 20cm (8in) square blue card, scored and folded to make 10 x 20cm (4 x 8in)
- Blue pearl and white card
- Blue striped paper
- Blue inkpad
- Footprint rubber stamps
- Blue embroidery thread
- 2 each of large, medium and small blue buttons

1 Using the blue inkpad, stamp a pair of feet on the white card (see page 22). Repeat to make a second pair. Leave to dry.

Quick & Clever

Use a stencil embossing tool to pick up a small amount of all-purpose sticky craft glue when applying it to the back of the buttons.

2 Cut around the feet stamps with a craft knife to make two 5.5cm (2⅛in) squares. Stick these squares on the blue pearl card using double-sided tape, and cut out with a craft knife so that a small border of blue is showing. Cut a 3 x 20cm (1¼ x 8in) panel of striped blue paper and stick to the front of the card using double-sided tape.

3 Position the stamped feet on the striped paper panel and stick in place using adhesive foam pads. Thread two strands of embroidery thread through each of the large buttons and tie in a double knot. Use single strands of thread for the medium and small buttons. Arrange the buttons at each end of the striped paper panel and attach using all-purpose sticky craft glue. Leave to dry.

Welcome Baby Bunny

Watch out for special stickers, like this adorable embossed rabbit, because they make the perfect centrepiece for greetings cards and are so easy to use. I've combined the sticker with some super embossed paper vellum to create a card that will warm the hearts of all new parents. Neutral soft colours are perfect for both boys and girls.

You will need

- 15cm (6in) soft green square card
- 10.5 x 15cm (4⅛ x 6in) paper vellum embossed with soft toys
- 7 x 8cm (2¾ x 3⅛in) cream card for mounting
- Embossed, three-dimensional rabbit sticker
- Green daisy brads

Quick & Clever

To ensure the brads lay flat without marking the card, place the card right side up and push down on the daisies to flatten the legs out at the back.

1 Stick a strip of double-sided tape on the back of the card close to the fold. Fold back 1cm (⅜in) of the paper vellum. Remove the backing paper from the tape, attach the vellum, so the strip is at the back and the panel folds to the front of the card, and firm down, ensuring that the top and bottom of the vellum line up with the card.

2 Secure the rabbit sticker in the centre of the cream card. Cut slits in the four corners, push the legs of the brads through to the back of the panel and open them out.

3 Stick strips of double-sided tape along all four edges of the cream panel. Position on the front of the card, half on the vellum and half on the card, then carefully remove the backing from the tape. In this way you secure the paper vellum as well as the rabbit.

heart-shaped buttons

coloured safety pins

silver hearts

duck punch

gingham bow

gingham papers

More bundles of joy

Gingham patterned papers, a duck punch and coloured safety pins were the materials that caught my eye and inspired me to make these cards to welcome or announce a special arrival. These fun cards also make perfect birthday cards for small children.

It's a Boy!

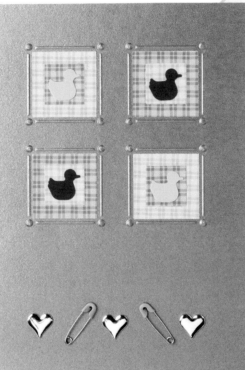

You will need

• A5 bought blank 4 square embossed blue card
• Blue and gold card
• Duck and medium and small square punches
• Yellow and blue gingham paper
• Silver hearts and safety pins

Punch two medium and two small squares out of yellow and blue gingham paper. Mount squares of yellow on blue and vice versa then secure in the embossed squares of the card using double-sided tape. Punch two ducks out of blue and gold card and stick on the gingham squares using a glue pen and again contrasting the colours. Add the silver hearts and safety pins along the bottom of the card using all-purpose sticky craft glue.

We have a girl
Baby's here
You have a boy
Dreams really do come true
What an extra special delivery!

A Precious Gift

Cut a 5 x 13cm (2 x 5⅛in) panel of yellow gingham paper and stick to the centre front of the folded card with double-sided tape. Punch and mount three small gingham squares on three medium punched gold card squares using double-sided tape. Punch three ducks from gold card and stick to the squares using a glue pen. Space the squares evenly down the gingham panel and secure with double-sided tape. Add a safety pin at the top and bottom of the card using all-purpose sticky craft glue. Stick a gingham bow to the folded edge of the card using all-purpose sticky craft glue.

You will need

- A5 folded gold card
- Yellow gingham paper
- Gold card
- Duck and medium and small square punches
- 2 yellow safety pins
- Yellow gingham ribbon

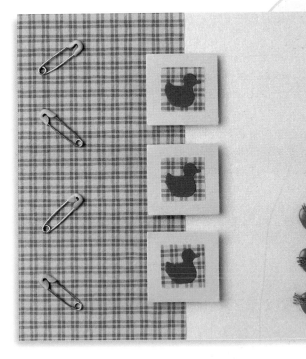

You will need

- 12cm (4¾in) square cream card
- Pink gingham paper
- Pink card
- Pink safety pins
- Duck and medium and small square punches
- Heart-shaped buttons
- Pink embroidery thread

A Special Little Girl

Stick a strip of pink gingham paper on the left side of the card front using double-sided tape and glue four safety pins down the edge using all-purpose sticky craft glue. Punch and mount three small pink gingham squares on three medium punched pink card squares using double-sided tape. Punch three pink ducks and stick these to the gingham squares using a glue pen. Arrange down the edge of the gingham strip and attach with adhesive foam pads. Tie two strands of pink embroidery thread through each button and stick to the right edge of the card.

More cracking cards!

A simple oval punch, perfect for creating egg shapes, was the inspiration for these fun Easter egg cards. Embellishments in tangy citrus colours are added for a fresh, spring finish.

Happy Easter

You will need

- 20 x 21cm (8 x 8¼in) white sparkle card, scored and folded to make 10 x 21cm (4 x 8¼in)
- White sparkle and green card
- Green striped paper
- Green daisy ribbon
- Green buttons
- Green embroidery thread
- Oval and daisy punch
- Flat-back crystals

Cut an 8 x 10cm (3⅛ x 4in) panel of green striped paper and stick to the front of the card with double-sided tape. Stick two lengths of ribbon to the top and bottom of the panel with double-sided tape. Tie a couple of strands of embroidery thread through each button and stick them to the corners of the ribbon using the all-purpose sticky craft glue. Use the oval punch to create an egg out of white sparkle card and decorate it with green punched daisies. Add flat-back crystals to the centres of the daisies. Attach the egg with adhesive foam pads.

Easter blessings

Springtime celebrations

Special Easter wishes

Have a hoppy Easter!

Hunt the Egg

Cut a 3 x 14.5cm (1¼ x 5¾in) strip of yellow daisy embossed paper and stick a strip of ribbon to it using double-sided tape. Stick to the front of the pocket. Cut a panel of yellow daisy paper slightly smaller than the card: mount on the card. Tie a couple of strands of embroidery thread through each button and glue to the corners of the card. Punch out three eggs using the oval punch and wrap a strip of ribbon around each egg, adding a bow to one. Punch daisies out of yellow paper and stick to the eggs, adding some flat-back crystals for sparkle. Attach the eggs to the card with adhesive foam pads.

You will need

- 15cm (6in) square cream pocket with card inside
- Cream card for punching
- Yellow daisy embossed paper
- Green daisy ribbon
- Green buttons
- Yellow embroidery thread
- Oval and daisy punch
- Yellow paper
- Flat-back crystals

You will need

- A5 folded cream card
- Yellow striped paper
- Medium, small and tiny orange buttons
- Yellow embroidery thread
- Yellow daisy embossed paper
- Yellow circle paper
- Oval punch
- Orange daisy ribbon

Ribbons and Bows

Cut a panel of yellow striped paper slightly smaller than the card and attach with double-sided tape. Tie a couple of strands of embroidery thread through four medium-sized buttons and glue one in each corner. Cut a thin strip of yellow daisy embossed paper and stick across the centre of the card with double-sided tape. Use the oval to punch an egg shape out of yellow circle paper; decorate with tiny and small threaded buttons and add a ribbon bow. Secure the egg using adhesive foam pads.

Halloween Magic

Mounting different coloured cards on top of each other is such a quick way to create an interesting effect on a greetings card. Add a spooky sticker or two and a touch of glitter glue and you have the perfect way to send Halloween wishes to friends and family.

You will need

- 15cm (6in) folded square cream card
- Purple, green and orange card
- Orange gingham ribbon
- Witch, spider and web stickers
- Glitter glue

1

Cut a 6.5 × 11.5cm (2⅝ × 4½in) panel from purple card, a 7 × 15cm (2¾ × 6in) panel from green card and an 8 × 15cm (3⅛ × 6in) panel from orange card. Select a witch sticker and stick it in the centre of the purple panel.

2

Use double-sided tape to mount the purple panel on the green panel, leaving a narrow border at the top and side edges. Wrap a length of orange gingham ribbon around the bottom of the green panel and tie in a knot at the front. Mount the green panel on the orange panel using double-sided tape.

3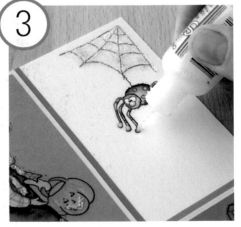

Cut a 6 × 2cm (2⅜ × ¾in) panel from orange card, a 6 × 2.5cm (2⅜ × 1in) panel from green card and a 6 × 3cm (2⅜ × 1¼in) panel from purple card. Mount orange on green and green on purple using double-sided sticky tape. Decorate the orange panel with spider stickers. Stick the witch and spider panels on the card, as shown, with double-sided tape. Stick a spider and web sticker to the top right-hand corner of the card and add glitter glue to the witch, spiders and web. Leave to dry.

⏰ *Quick & Clever*

Use your fingernail to rub around the edge of the stickers – this will take the shine away and ensure they are stuck down well.

spider confetti

witch die cut
shape and
name card

gold card

More spooky fun

Super gold mirror card, spooky spider confetti and a wonderful die cut witch shape were the basis for these themed Halloween cards. I've made a party invitation, name card for seating, a tag that is perfect for a trick 'n' treat bag and an original spider decoration for drinking straws

Invitation
Mount the witch shape on to purple, green and orange card using the glue pen and cutting each one out carefully with scissors. Glue the witch to the front of the triangle card, and add a couple of confetti spiders. Highlight with glitter glue.

Tag
Trace around the tag template (see page 106), transfer to gold card and cut out. Punch a hole for attaching the tag, then glue on some purple and black spider confetti to decorate. Highlight the spiders with glitter glue.

Name Card
Mount a witch die cut name card on to purple, green and orange card using the glue pen and cutting each one out carefully using scissors. Cut an 18 × 12.5cm (7 × 5in) piece of gold card and score and fold to make it 9 × 12.5cm (3½ × 5in). Glue the witch name card to the gold card and add some spider confetti in purple and black. Decorate the witches and outline the name tag with glitter glue.

You will need
- 14.5 × 16 × 16cm (5¾ × 6¼ × 6¼in) bought blank gold mirror triangle card
- Orange, green, gold and purple card
- Witch die cut shape and name card
- Spider confetti
- Glitter glue
- Hole punch

Straw Decoration
Cut a small oblong of gold card and punch two holes at each end. Stick a confetti spider between the holes. Thread the straw through the punched holes. Decorate the spiders with glitter glue.

Happy trick-or-treating

Best witches!

Happy Halloween

Happy Booday to you!

Party time for witches and wizards

Instant Celebrations

Sometimes you need a card for a more unusual celebration – such as graduation day or to wish someone bon voyage – here are some inspirational ideas to mark those occasions. Also included are extra designs for birthdays and Christmas, which are the two celebrations we most frequently need cards for. There are some lovely birthday cards for men – who are always difficult to please! – and women, boys and girls, and babies. Some designs, which I have suggested could be used as a thank you or congratulations card, could equally well be used to mark birthdays.

You will need

- 12cm (4¾in) square copper card
- Antique map paper
- Extra copper card
- Antique travel tag stickers
- Hole punch
- String

Bon Voyage

This card is perfect for friends or family who are going on that once-in-a-lifetime holiday or moving overseas, or even for a child who is taking their first solo trip.

Cut a square of antique map paper slightly smaller than your copper card and stick it to the front of the card with double-sided tape, leaving a border all round. Stick the tag stickers to copper card and cut out leaving a border of copper showing. Punch holes in the tags then thread them on to string and wrap it all the way around the front of the card. Knot the string above the top tag. Stick the tags to the card using adhesive foam pads, positioned each side of the string.

The Graduate

Congratulations, you've passed! Mark exam passes, degree graduations or any occasion when academic achievement needs to be recognized.

Cut a square of blue card big enough to take the mortar board and stick in place. Mount on to gold card with double-sided tape and trim, leaving a narrow border. Stick in the centre top of the main card. Cut a strip of blue card the width of the opal card, and add the scroll and two punched out gold stars. Mount this panel on to gold card, leaving a narrow border showing at the top and bottom, and stick to the lower section of the card.

You will need

- A4 (US letter) opal card, halved then scored and folded to make A5
- Blue and gold card
- Mortar board and scroll sticker
- Star punch

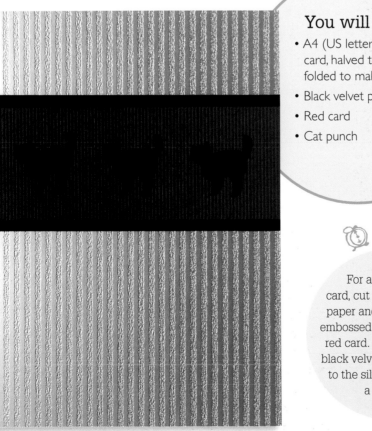

You will need

- A4 (US letter) silver ridged card, halved then scored and folded to make A5
- Black velvet paper
- Red card
- Cat punch

Good Luck

Make sure friends and family know that you are wishing them all the best in their endeavours with this lucky black cat card.

Punch three cats out of black velvet paper. Cut a panel of red card the same width as the silver card and big enough to hold the punched cats. Stick the cats to the panel using a glue pen. Cut a panel of black velvet paper slightly wider than the red panel, and stick the red panel on top using double-sided tape. Stick to the top front of the silver card.

Quick & Clever

For an even faster card, cut a square of silver paper and stick inside the embossed square on a blank red card. Punch a cat from black velvet paper and stick to the silver square using a glue pen.

Tartan Greetings

Perfect for a traditional Hogmanay, this design is fitting for all those who enjoy New Year celebrations Scots' style!

Cut a strip of tartan paper to cover half of the red card and stick on with double-sided tape. Cut four holly leaves using the die and die cutter and gold mirror card, and stick two on the tartan paper and two on the red card using a glue pen. Glue red and green flat-back crystals in the holly berry holes and leave to dry.

You will need

- 15cm (6in) square folded red card
- Tartan paper
- Gold mirror card
- Holly die
- Sizzix die cutter
- Red and green flat-back crystals

You will need

- 15cm (6in) square folded black card
- Christmas trees rubber stamp
- Gold card which is black on the reverse
- Gold inkpad
- Star punch

Star Topped Trees

This rubber stamped card is perfect for mass production, which is a necessity at Christmas.

Stamp the Christmas tree design in gold on to an 8 × 6.5cm (3⅛ × 2½in) panel of black card. Layer on to slightly larger panels of gold and black card with double-sided tape, then mount on to a panel of gold card leaving a slightly larger border. Finally, stick the mounted image to the folded card with double-sided tape.

Snowy Wishes

Delight friends and family with this clever centre-opening card.

Take a snowflake peel-off sticker and stick it on one of the front sides of the card. Take a little colour from the inkpad and sponge over the top of the peel-off sticker. Lift the peel-off sticker and move it around the card, sponging on colour, until the card is covered with a snowflake design. Leave to dry. Add flat-back crystals to the embossed snowflake using a glue pen and leave to dry.

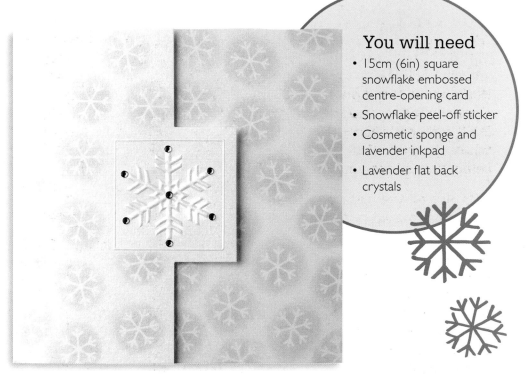

You will need

- 15cm (6in) square snowflake embossed centre-opening card
- Snowflake peel-off sticker
- Cosmetic sponge and lavender inkpad
- Lavender flat back crystals

You will need

- 16 x 17.5cm (6¼ x 7in) white card, scored and folded to make 8 x 17.5cm (3⅛ x 7in)
- Rub on snowflake panel
- Wooden lollipop (popsicle) stick
- Blue flat-back crystals

Yuletide Greetings

Send Christmas or New Year greetings with this sparkling snowflake motif.

Place the rub on snowflake panel down the centre of the folded white card and rub down with a wooden lollipop stick. Stick flat-back crystals to the centres of the snowflakes with all-purpose sticky craft glue and leave to dry.

Celtic Knot

This is the perfect card for any man in your life to say 'congratulations' and to celebrate birthdays and retirements. It also works for all people of all ages and all sexes – a good all-rounder!

Place the rubber stamp, rubber side up on an ironing board. Place the velvet paper, velvet side down on top of the rubber stamp. Turn the steam off on the iron and set to velvet heat setting. Place the iron over the velvet paper and the rubber stamp, hold it there and count to 10 slowly, before removing. Cut around the Celtic knot using deckle-edged scissors. Mount the blue velvet paper on blue pearlized card and then on silver mirror card. Stick to the main card using double-sided tape.

You will need
- 15cm (6in) square folded white card
- Dark blue velvet paper
- Blue pearlized card
- Silver mirror card
- Celtic knot rubber stamp
- Iron
- Deckle-edged scissors

You will need
- 15cm (6in) folded square green card
- Line green, purple and cream card
- Skateboarding sticker
- Glitter glue

Action Boy

Teenagers – and boys in particular – are really hard to make cards for so these skateboarding stickers are brilliant.

Stick the skateboard sticker to an 8 x 8.5cm (3⅛ x 3⅜in) panel of lime green card then layer on to slightly larger squares of purple and cream card. Add glitter glue to highlight areas of the design. Cut a 4.5 x 15cm (1¾ x 6in) strip of lime green card and stick across the centre of the folded card with double-sided tape. Stick the skateboard panel to the card with adhesive foam pads.

You will need

- 20 × 21cm (8 × 8¼in) square bronze card, scored and folded to make 10 × 21cm (4 × 8¼in)
- Golf bag sticker
- Bronze card which is blue on the reverse
- Square corner cutter

Have a Swinging Birthday

The perfect way to send birthday wishes to a keen golfer.

Stick the golf bag sticker to a 6 × 15cm (2⅜ × 6in) panel of bronze card and punch each corner with the square corner cutter. Mount on to a slightly larger panel of blue card using double-sided tape. Attach to the front of the folded card with adhesive foam pads.

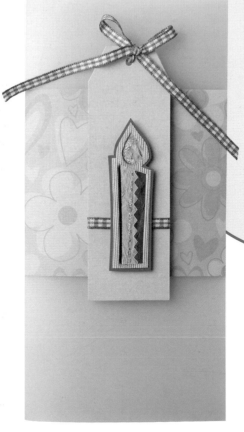

You will need

- 20 × 21cm (8 × 8¼in) pink plasma card, scored and folded to give 10 × 21cm (4 × 8¼in)
- Pink card
- 4 × 12cm (1½ × 4¾in) pink tag
- 10 × 9cm (4 × 3½in) panel of pink patterned paper
- Candle print
- Pink gingham ribbon
- Glitter glue

Make a Wish

Every child associates candles with birthdays so this is the ideal card for a toddler – it also makes a lovely Christening card.

Cut the printed candle design out, stick to pink card and cut out, leaving a narrow border. Stick ribbon around the bottom half of the tag with double-sided sticky tape and stick the candle to the tag, on top of the ribbon, using adhesive foam pads. Add glitter glue to the candle. Stick the patterned pink paper to the plasma card with double-sided tape and attach the tag on top using adhesive foam pads.

Teddy is Tops

A wonderful way to celebrate a child's first birthday. Add their name for a personal touch.

Attach the teddy sticker to a 9cm (3½in) square of lilac card and tear around the edges. Cut a slightly larger square of mulberry paper and, using a wet paintbrush, tease the edges apart to give a wispy look. Use double-sided tape to stick the mounted teddy to the mulberry paper and then spray adhesive to adhere the mulberry paper to a 12.5cm (5in) square of mauve card. Mount again on to a slightly larger square of purple metallic card, then to the main card using double-sided tape.

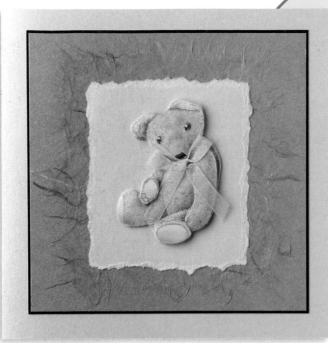

You will need

- 15cm (6in) folded square lilac card
- Mauve and lilac card
- Purple metallic card
- 3D teddy sticker
- Purple mulberry paper
- Spray adhesive

Birthday Bonanza

Balloons bring a smile to everyone's face, even that hard to please teenager. This card makes a great party invitation and works well as a congratulations card too.

Punch a balloon from coral card. Bend and shape a length of copper wire, adding beads as you go. Wind the wire round the bottom of the balloon then stick the balloon to a 5.5 × 15cm (2⅛in × 6in) panel of copper card with adhesive foam pads. Layer on to a slightly larger panel of bronze card. Cut a 3.5 × 21cm (1⅜ × 8¼in) panel of copper card and position down the centre front of the coral card with double-sided tape. Punch out small coral daisies and tiny peach daisies, and stick to the card using a glue pen. Add beads to the centres of all the daisies using all-purpose sticky craft glue and leave to dry.

You will need

- 20 × 21cm (8 × 8¼in) coral card, scored and folded to give 10 × 21cm (4 × 8¼in)
- Coral, bronze, copper, and peach card
- Copper wire
- Beads
- Balloon punch
- Daisy punch small and tiny

Say it with a Flower

If you are short on time but want to impress, these stunning beaded stickers are the answer. This is a card for girls who love anything that sparkles!

Mount the beaded sticker on a 6 x 10cm (2⅜ x 4in) panel of cream card and stick to a slightly larger panel of pink card with double-sided tape. Cut an 8.5 x 12.5cm (3⅜ x 5in) panel of pale pink card and punch each corner with the square corner cutter. Stick the mounted sticker to the pale pink card then to the main card using double-sided tape.

You will need

- A5 pink card, scored and folded to give 10.5 x 14.8cm (4⅛ x 5¾in)
- Sparkler flower sticker
- Cream, pink and pale pink card
- Square corner cutter

You will need

- 12cm (4¾in) folded square mauve card
- Lilac and pink card and purple metallic card
- Butterfly sticker
- Seed beads

Butterfly Wishes

Pretty coloured card and a fantastic dimensional beaded sticker are a great combination to send girly birthday wishes.

Stick the butterfly sticker to a 6cm (2⅜in) square of lilac card, then to slightly larger squares of pink, lilac card and purple metallic card. Add seed beads to the corners of the layers. Stick the layered panel to the front of the card with adhesive foam pads.

4th of July

This funky card is perfect for celebrating Independence Day with sparkle and style.

Tear five thin strips of white card and space evenly down the folded red card. Secure with double-sided tape. Trace off the heart template (see page 106), transfer to the back of the blue card, and tear out the shape. Punch out red stars and stick to the blue heart with a glue pen. Mount the heart on the card using double-sided tape.

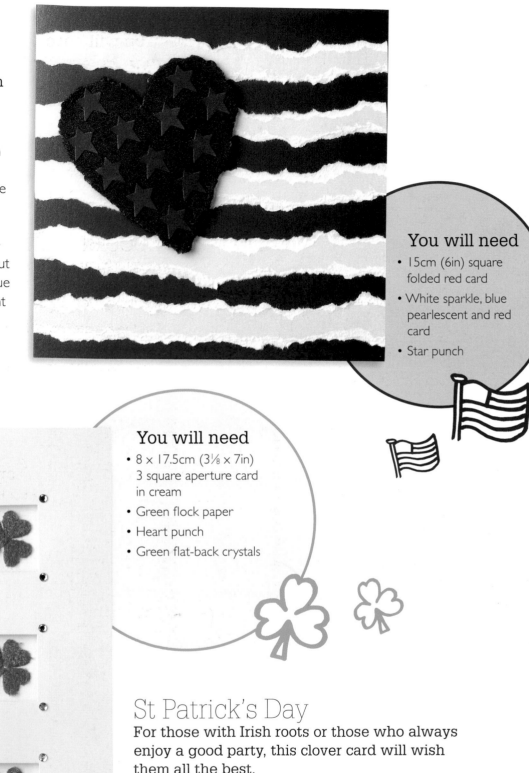

You will need
- 15cm (6in) square folded red card
- White sparkle, blue pearlescent and red card
- Star punch

You will need
- 8 x 17.5cm (3⅛ x 7in) 3 square aperture card in cream
- Green flock paper
- Heart punch
- Green flat-back crystals

St Patrick's Day

For those with Irish roots or those who always enjoy a good party, this clover card will wish them all the best.

Punch nine hearts from the green flock paper. Working from the front of the card, arrange them in clover leaf shapes inside each aperture. Cut thin stems from the flock paper and use a glue pen to stick all the pieces down. Highlight the corner of each square with a flat-back crystal.

You will need

- 15cm (6in) square folded white card
- Sheet of London acetate motifs
- Spray adhesive
- Tickets and mementoes

Special Memories

Remind someone of a special trip you've enjoyed together, such as a honeymoon or exciting weekend.

Cut the acetate motifs from the sheet. Arrange the motifs, tickets and mementoes in a pleasing design, then stick to the card using spray adhesive.

Thank You

This simple design is perfect for saying thanks, but also get well or congratulations.

Tear a piece of yellow paper vellum to fit inside the embossed rectangle and stick in place with the glue pen. Add the daisy-in-a-vase sticker to the centre of the vellum.

You will need

- 8 x 17.5cm (3⅛ x 7in) cream card with embossed rectangle
- Yellow paper vellum
- Daisy-in-a-vase sticker

Templates

All templates are full size

Hammer Home Good Wishes
(see page 43)

In the Bag
(see page 43)

More Spooky Fun
(see page 82)

4th of July
(see page 104)

3.5cm

Sealed with a Kiss
(see page 55)

3cm

5.5cm

5.5cm

3.5cm

Heartfelt
(see page 59)

Ten Tiny Toes
(see page 71)

Sent with Love
(see page 62)

Cut away

Cut

Fold

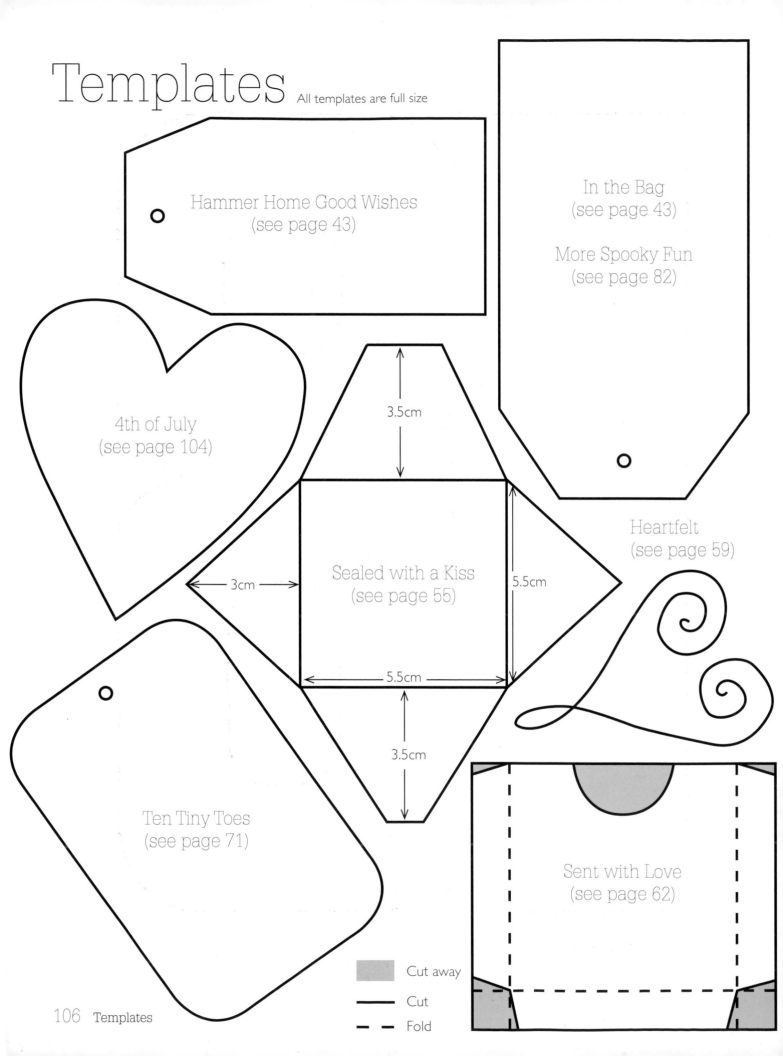

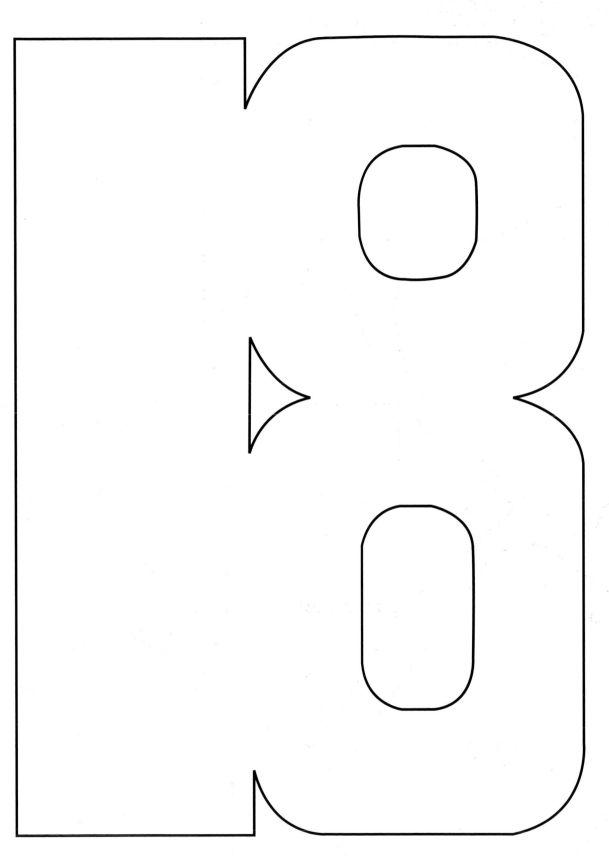

18 Today (see page 51)

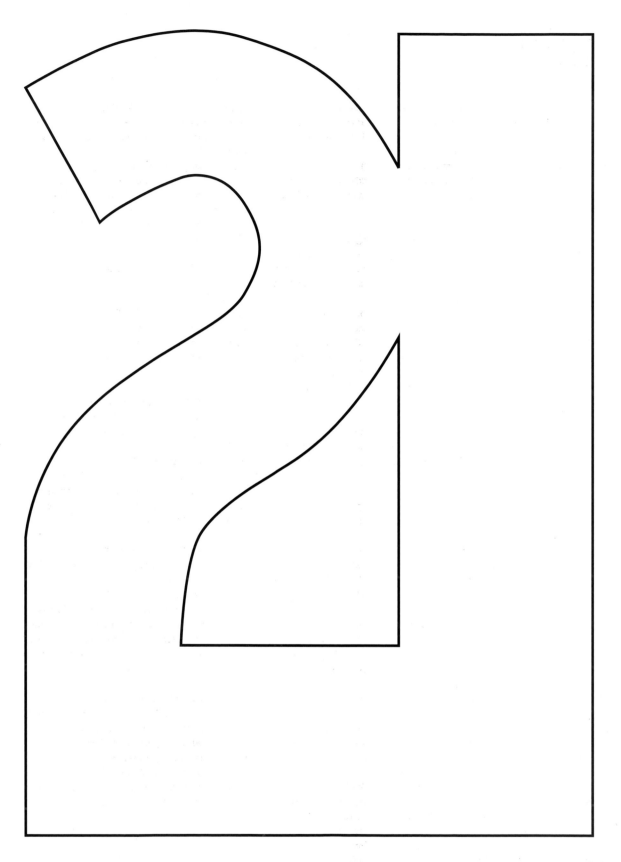

Star Spangled Celebration (see page 51)

Materials

GET READY (PAGES 10–33)

Sizzix and Side Kick machines, paddle punch system (pages 12–13): *The Craft Bug*
Craft heat tool (page 22): *Creative Pastimes*
Candy Cane Wand for hot fix crystals (page 23): *The Finishing Touch*

All cards and paper used are from *Craftwork Cards Limited*, unless otherwise stated

BIRTHDAY CHARM (pages 36–37)

Background papers, frame and tags: *Ki Memories, from Creative Pastimes*. Handbag and shoe charms, crystals: *Craftwork Cards Limited*. Flower shaped brads: *Scrapmagic*. Sheer ribbon: *Crafty Ribbons*

More for the girls (pages 38–39)

Frames, blocks, circles and icicle flowers: *Ki Memories, from Creative Pastimes*. Crystals: *Craftwork Cards Limited*. Flower shaped brads: *Making Memories, from The Scrapbook House*. Flower and Butterfly Stamps: *Hero Arts, from F W Bramwells*

A BIRTHDAY CATCH (pages 40–41)

Embossed card and vellum: *Once Upon a Stamp*
Brads: *Scrapbook House*

More for the guys (page 42–43)

Floorboard background paper and DIY charms: *Creative Pastimes*. Screw Head Snaps: *Making Memories, from The Scrapbook House*

HAPPY BIRTHDAY DUDE (pages 44–45)

All rubber stamps used: *S for Stamps*. Art Kure Brushes: *Art Kure*

More cool kids (pages 46–47)

Balloon punch and tiny star punch: *The Art of Crafts*
Sheer ribbon: *Crafty Ribbons*. Silver wire and bugle beads: *Creative Pastimes*

COMING OF AGE (pages 48–49)

Dress and shoe rubber stamps: *Impression Obsession, from Stamps n Memories*. Art Kure Brushes: *Art Kure*
Perfect Positioner: *The London Bead Co.*

More special birthdays (pages 50–51)

Explosion rubber stamp: *by Denami, from Stamp Addicts*. 21 and 18 Confetti: *Creative Pastimes*. Card matt for shaker card: *Craftwork Cards Limited*

HEARTS AND ROSES (pages 52–53)

Serviette: *supermarkets and garden centres*. Gold metal hearts: *Scrapyard 329, from Craftwork Cards Limited*

More loving wishes (pages 54–55)

Lip rubber stamp: *Rubber Stampede, from Creative Pastimes*. Crystals, heart shaped gems and vellum: *Craftwork Cards Limited*. Sheer ribbon: *Crafty Ribbons*

WEDDING ELEGANCE (pages 56–57)

Paddle punch systems and paddle punch heart die: *Sizzix, from The Craft Bug*. Flat backed crystals: *Craftwork Cards Limited*

More romance (pages 58-59)

Paddle punch system and paddle punch heart die: *Sizzix, from The Craft Bug*. Crystals: *Craftwork Cards Limited*

ANNIVERSARY CHARM (pages 60-61)

Pink Frame: *Ki Memories, from Creative Pastimes*.
Heart locket and key charms: *Craftwork Cards Limited*
Pink sheer ribbon: *Crafty Ribbons*. Heart shaped brads: *Hobby Horse Crafts*

More anniversary ideas (pages 62–63)

Vellum papers in gold, silver and red: *Craftwork Cards Limited*. Françoise Read Champagne Glasses rubber stamp, embossing ink pad, gold, silver and red embossing powder, heart peel-off stickers in gold, silver and red: *Creative Pastimes*. Sheer Ribbon: *Crafty Ribbons*

KEYS TO THE DOOR (pages 64–65)

Embossing board: *The Craft Cottage*. Metal tag: *Scrap Ease, from Craftwork Cards*. Key Punch: *Creative Pastimes*. Brads: *Scrap Magic*

More happy homes (pages 66–67)

Door peel-off stickers, flower pot punch and all flower and daisy punches: *Art of Crafts*

THE PITTER PATTER… (pages 68–69)

Feet rubber stamps by Inkadinkado: *F W Bramwell*.
Patterned paper and threads: *Making Memories, from The Scrapbook House*. Buttons: *Lasting Impressions, from Creative Pastimes*

More new arrivals (pages 70–71)

Pink stripped papers: *SEI, from Craftwork Cards Limited*. Metal pram, duck, bottle and tag: *Scrap Easi, from Craftwork Cards Limited. .* Gingham ribbon from *Crafty Ribbons*. Tiny buttons: *Creative Pastimes*.
Heart shaped brads: *Hobby Horse Crafts*

WELCOME BABY BUNNY (pages 72–73)

Embossed vellum and embossed 3D stickers: *K&Co, from Once Upon a Stamp*. Tiny daisy brads: *Bazzill Basics, from Scrap Magic*

More bundles of joy (pages 74–75)

Duck punch, gingham patterned paper, buttons and threads: *Creative Pastimes*. Safety pins: *Making Memories, from The Scrapbook House*
Metal hearts: *Scrapyard 329, from Craftwork Cards Limited*. Gingham ribbon: *Crafty Ribbons*

EASTER PARADE (pages 76–77)

All rubber stamps: *S for Stamps*. Oval punch: *Creative Pastimes*. Gingham ribbon: *Crafty Ribbons*. Crystals: *Craftwork Cards Limited*

More cracking cards! (pages 78–79)

Oval punch for eggs, buttons and threads: *Creative Pastimes*. Tiny daisy punch: *The Art of Crafts*. Daisy ribbon: *Crafty Ribbons*. Flat-back crystals: *Craftwork Cards Limited*. Embossed yellow daisy paper: *Hobby Horse Crafts*.

HALLOWEEN MAGIC (pages 80–81)

Witch stickers: *The Paper Trail Scrapbook Company*.
Ribbon: *Crafty Ribbons*

More spooky fun (pages 82–83)

Gold mirror triangle cards: *Craftwork Cards Limited*.
Spider confetti: *Creative Pastimes*. Die cut witch and witch name placecard: *The Paper Trail Scrapbook Company*

SNOWTIME SPARKLE (pages 84–85)

Quilled snowflake sticker: *F W Bramwell*. Snowflake rubber stamp: *S for Stamps*. Flat-back crystals: *Craftwork Cards Limited*

More festive treats (86–67)

Sizzix die cutting machine and Sizzlits Christmas dies: *Sizzix, from The Craft Bug*. Silver wire and beads: *Creative Pastimes*. Tartan paper: *Scrap Magic*. Tree embossed card: *Craftwork Cards*

SEASONS GREETINGS (pages 88–89)

Sizzix snowflake embossing sleeve: *The Craft Bug*. Flat-back crystals: *Craftwork Cards Limited*

More winter wishes (pages 90–91)

Snowflake enamelled stickers and crystals: *Craftwork Cards Limited*. Silver snowflake peel-off stickers, blue glitter snowflake rub ons and snowflake punch: *Paper Shapers, from Creative Pastimes*. Vellum tag stickers and snowflake stickers: *Scrap Magic*

SHOW YOU CARE (pages 92–93)

Rubber stamp Hero Arts: *F W Bramwells*. Chalks by Pebbles Inc: *Crafts U Love*. Flat-back crystals: *Craftwork Cards Limited*. Sheer ribbon: *Crafty Ribbons*

More caring thoughts (pages 94–95)

Sizzix embossing sleeve lily: *Sizzix, from The Craft Bug*.
Chalks: *Pebbles Inc. from Crafts U Love*. Sheer ribbon: *Crafty Ribbons*. Crystals: *Craftwork Cards Limited*

Suppliers

Art Kure
Hayloft Studios
Ballemarsh Barton
Kingsteignton Road
Chudleigh
Devon TQ13 OAJ
tel: 01626 859 100
www.Art-Kure.com

The Art of Crafts Limited
101 Lynchford Road
North Camp
Farnborough
Hants GU14 6ET
tel: 01252 377677
www.art-of-craft.co.uk

F W Bramwell & Co Limited
Old Empress Mill
Empress Street
Colne
Lancashire B8 9UU
tel: 01282 860388
www.bramwellcrafts.co.uk

The Craft Bug
26 West View
Chirk
Wrexham LL14 5HN
tel: 01691 774778
www.thecraftbug.co.uk

The Craft Cottage
Unit 5a Tonedale Business Park
Millstream Gardens
Wellington
Somerset TA21 0AW
tel: 01823 669055

Crafts U Love
Three Pines
170 Balcombe Road
Horley
Surrey RH6 9ER
tel: 01293 776 465
www.craftsulove.co.uk

Craftwork Cards Limited
Unit 2 The Moorings
Waterside Road
Stourton
Leeds LS10 1RW
tel: 0113 276 5713
www.craftworkcards.co.uk

Crafty Ribbons
3 Beechwood Clump Farm
Blandford
Dorset
tel: 01258 455889

Creative Pastimes
Boulthurst Farm
Pains Hill
Limpsfield
Surrey RH8 0RG
tel: 01883 730033
www.creativepastimes.co.uk

The Finishing Touch
PO Box 6812
Grantham NG31 7QR
tel: 01476 593400
email: Elaine@diamantedesigns.com

Hobby Horse Crafts
Gardens Cottage
Main Road
Elvaston
Derbyshire
tel: 01332 572 904

The London Bead Co.
339 Kentish Town Road
London NW5 2TJ
tel: 0870 203 2323
www.londonbeadco.co.uk

Once Upon a Stamp
Unit 6 Cannon Court
Beetwell Street
Chesterfield
Derbyshire S40 1SH
tel: 01246 278 448
www.onceuponastamp.co.uk

The Paper Trail Scrapbook Company
2 Providence Place
Bridlington
East Yorkshire YO15 2QW
tel: 01262 601 770
www.goscrapbook.co.uk

The Scrapbook House
Unit 9 Cromwell Business Park
Chipping Norton
Oxon OX7 5SR
tel: 08707 707717
www.thescrapbookhouse.com

Scrapmagic
56 Brighton Road
Surbiton
Surrey KT6 5PL
tel: 0208 390 3090
www.scrapmagic.com

S for Stamps
15 Southport Road
Rutherglen
Glasgow G73 1SP
tel: 0141 613 2680
www.sforstamps.co.uk

Stamp Addicts
Unit 5a Lyon Close
Woburn Road Industrial Estate
Kempston
Bedford MK42 7SB
tel: 01234 855 833
www.stampaddictsshop.co.uk

Stamps n Memories
36 Dunn Crescent
Kintbury
Hungerford
Berkshire RH17 9UH
tel: 01488 658 728

Acknowledgments

Mervyn, Matthew and Owen – you all put up with so much mess, lack of meals and attention from me while I write my books. I could not do it without your love and support. Thank you.

Mum – you always encourage me, support me and above all else, thank you for all the ironing you did while I wrote this book.

A HUGE thank you to Sue and Richard at Craftwork Cards for generously supplying all the cards used in this book. You both know how much I love all your products. Sue you are so creative and that's the reason the company is where it is today. Thank you for sharing your creativity with me and feeding me with inspiration. You are both such good friends and we do make such a brilliant team! Thank you to the rest of the extremely efficient team – Steffi, Julie, Sonya, Michelle, Yvonne, Nicola, Simon, Steve and Rose, you always make me feel so welcome and so much a part of the team.

Melanie – you always encourage and inspire me when the creativity stops flowing. Your belief in me commercially never ceases to amaze me. Thank you.

I have made so many good friends over the years while card making, too many to mention you all by name, but all customers who have attended a workshop have helped to develop my style a little further. Some very special friends include: Sue Taylor, Melanie Hendrick, Caroline (Caz) Counsell, Corinne Amos, Annie Winch, Kim Reygate, Anna Flanders, Dawn Petler, Paula Pascuel and Françoise Read.

Thank you to all the shops that have supported me with products for this book. I really appreciate your generosity. (See pages 109–110 for useful names, addresses and contact numbers.) A special thank you to Paul at the Carp Shop for the loan of your fabulous flies.

Anna – thank you for taking all the notes again and making the typing of the step-by-step projects so easy. Your expert eye was also a real help with the photography.

Ginette – you have done it again! The photography is quite simply stunning and makes the book; you just want to turn the page to see what's coming next. Your eye for detail and patience make you an absolute pleasure to work with and I hope to work with you again very soon. Thank you.

Cheryl – you have been a great commissioning editor, so easy to work with and always there to help. I hope to work with you again soon. Thank you.

Jenny – always so helpful, so efficient and always on hand for any questions I have. You are brilliant, thank you for everything.

Pru – you have done a great job with the designing of the book and have been so helpful whenever I have called you.

Carey – you worked wonders on my words and are a delight to work with. Thank you.

I also want to thank everyone who buys a copy of this book, without you there would be no book. I hope you get inspiration from all the ideas and that the book has you reaching for your crafting tools. Enjoy!

About the author

Julie Hickey is a successful card maker, workshop tutor and author. She is involved with running the Craftwork Cards Card Club, a mail-order club that supplies projects, newsletters and materials to over 5,000 members in the UK, USA and Europe. Julie also demonstrates around the UK at all the major paper crafting, rubber stamp and scrap booking shows. She is a regular contributor to *Crafts Beautiful* and *Quick n Crafty* and has appeared on the Create and Craft shopping channel on Sky TV.

This is Julie's fourth book, and her second with David and Charles. Julie's first book book with David and Charles, *Quick & Clever Handmade Cards*, is a best-seller. She lives with her husband Mervyn and two sons, Matthew and Owen, in Horley, Surrey.

Index

Same-sex Marriag

LOUISE SPILSBURY

Published in 2013 by Wayland
Copyright © 2013 Wayland

Wayland
338 Euston Road
London NW1 3BH

Wayland Australia
Level 17/207 Kent Street
Sydney NSW 2000

Editor: Nicola Edwards
Designer: Rita Storey

British Library Cataloguing in Publication
data

Spilsbury, Louise.
    Same-sex marriage. -- (Ethical debates)
    1. Same-sex marriage--Moral and ethical
aspects--Juvenile literature. 2. Civil
unions--Moral and ethical aspects--
Juvenile literature.
    I. Title II. Series
    173-dc22

ISBN 978 0 7502 7957 4

10 9 8 7 6 5 4 3 2 1

Printed in China

Wayland is a division of Hachette Children's
Books,
an Hachette UK company.
www.hachette.co.uk

Picture acknowledgements:
The author and publisher would like to
thank the following agencies for allowing
these pictures to be reproduced:
Cover: iStock/Martin Purmensky; title page:
iStock © Anne Clark; pp4-5 Getty Images;
p6 iStock © Christopher Futcher; p7 iStock
© Anne Clark; p8 © Jon Bower London /
Alamy; p9 Shutterstock/M Reel; p10 © A
Eastland / Alamy; p11 Getty Images; p12
Shutterstock/Kimberly Hall; p13
iStock/Martin Purmensky; p14
Shutterstock/get4net; p15 Shutterstock/
Monkey Business Images; p16 John
Birdsall/John Birdsall/Press Association
Images; p17 Halldor Kolbeins/ AFP/Getty
Images; p18 Pedro Armestre/AFP/Getty
Images; p19 Eduardo Verdugo/AP/Press
Association Images; p20 Shutterstock/
marcokenya; p21Getty Images; p22
Shutterstock Benjamin Loo; p23
Shutterstock Rebecca Photography; p24
AP/Press Association Images; pp25-26
AFP/Getty Images; p27 Darren
McCollester/Getty Images; p28 AP Photo/Mel
Evans; p30 Douglas C. Pizac/AP/Press
Association Images; p31 STR/AFP/Getty
Images; p32 iStock/ Stratesigns Inc; p33
iStock/RonTech2000; p34 iStock/Catherine
Yeulet; p35 AP Photo/Mike Derer; p36
Gareth Fuller/PA Wire/Press Association
Images; p38 Getty Images; p39 Kaveh
Kazemi/Getty Images; p40 iStock/Konstantin
Goldenberg; p41 Shutterstock Meiqianbao;
p42 Seth Wenig/AP/Press Association
Images; p43 Schalk van Zuydam/AP/Press
Association Images; p44 Wikimedia
Commons/ Beatrice Murch;p45 Alex
Wong/Getty Images

About the Consultant: Jayne Wright has
worked in Education for over 15 years,
including as a teacher, a citizenship
consultant to schools and as Regional
Adviser and National Assessor on the
National PSHE Continuing Professional
Development Programme.

contents

Real-life case study

This real-life case study highlights some of the issues that surround the debate on same-sex marriage.

case study

Same-sex marriage in California

In June 2008 the state of California in the USA passed a law allowing same-sex marriage for the first time. Same-sex marriage is the marriage between two men or two women. The first couple to be wed after the law was passed were the lead plaintiffs in the case that changed the law, Robin Tyler and Diane Olson. It was a significant moment in America – the ceremony was shown on three local TV networks, and there were more media people than guests at Beverly Hills City Hall, Los Angeles where the white-tuxedo wearing couple were married.

The two women had been together for 15 years and had known each other for 35 and they had been applying for a marriage licence for 7 years before their wish was finally granted. Supporters of same-sex marriage outside the hall waved rainbow flags and a sign saying simply: 'Finally.' However, even on Olson and Tyler's happy day there were several angry protesters carrying banners with slogans like 'Legalising gay marriage is legalising sin' and the fierce debate around same-sex marriage in California continued.

▼ US and world press and protestors crowd around Robin Tyler (left) and Diane Olson at their wedding in June 2008.

Within a year Tyler and Olson were faced with the prospect of their union – and that of thousands of other homosexual couples – being annulled, and their status as a married couple being taken away from them. In May 2009 the Supreme Court of California met to decide to uphold Proposition 8, a ballot in which a small majority of Californians had voted for a measure that stipulated: 'only marriage between a man and a woman is valid or recognised in California'.

The court's decision did not affect those already married, such as Tyler and Olsen. They, and around 18,000 other homosexual couples who had been married during the six-month period when same-sex marriage was allowed, could stay married. However, the court upheld the ban on any new same-sex weddings. Tyler and Olson and other married homosexual couples in California now lived in a state where same-sex marriage was officially illegal.

In February 2012 a federal appeals court ruled that Proposition 8 violated the Constitution by discriminating against gay and lesbian people. In March 2013 the US Supreme Court heard arguments for and against the legality of Proposition 8 and could make a nationwide law about same-sex marriage.

viewpoints

'I feel fabulous. I feel in love, I feel giddy, I feel happy. It's like it's not real.'
Robin Tyler on her wedding day

'Boys do not marry boys, girls do not marry girls, they never have, whatever they want to do, this is not marriage.'
A protester, who gave his name as John, on Tyler and Olson's wedding day

▼ In August 2010 supporters of same-sex marriage in California, including Olsen and Tyler, celebrated after a federal US judge declared that Proposition 8 was unconstitutional.

Proposition 8
Born 11/4/08
Dead & Buried 8/4/10

& JUSTICE
ALL

CHAPTER 1

Same-sex relationships

Most people are attracted to members of the opposite sex. Most boys or men are attracted to girls and women, and vice versa. While heterosexual relationships like these are most common, there are also many men and women who are attracted to someone of the same sex as themselves. They are known as homosexual or gay, and homosexual women may refer to themselves as lesbians.

Sexual orientation

Some people say that they knew they were homosexual from a young age; for others it is a realisation that comes more gradually. For teenagers the sex hormones that cause puberty and an increase in sexual drive or urges can make it a confusing time. Many people find that they are attracted to members of the same sex for a while and this is perfectly normal. It doesn't mean they are homosexual, though it may do. No one knows what makes people heterosexual, homosexual or even bisexual. Whether someone finally realises they are attracted to the same or to the opposite sex, they are experiencing a normal sexual orientation.

▼ The teenage years are a period of self-discovery about many attitudes and beliefs, and also awareness of sexual orientations.

Coming out

When someone decides to tell other people that they are homosexual it is known as 'coming out'. Some people find coming out a positive experience, because they can finally express their true feelings. However, it can be a difficult time for many others as a lot of people refuse to accept homosexuality. Prejudice against homosexual people and homosexuality is called homophobia. Like many people who are outside the 'norm' at school, college and beyond, some homosexuals face varying degrees of bullying, from name-calling and the frequent use of words like gay being used as insults to more violent forms of physical abuse.

Like other people who are bullied, homosexuals who are bullied are less likely to do well at school, may become depressed, or harm themselves. According to Stonewall, a charity that campaigns for a stop to homophobic abuse, almost half of those who have encountered such abuse consider self-harm or even suicide.

▼ 'Coming out' is when someone publicly identifies themself as a homosexual.

Attitudes

People's attitudes to homosexuality vary widely. In some countries such as Nigeria and Iran, coming out is incredibly dangerous because homosexual behaviour carries the death penalty. In other places, such as Europe and North America, homosexuality is legal and homophobia against the law. However, even in these places, intolerance is still widespread and homosexual people have different legal rights to heterosexual people and issues such as same-sex marriage are still hotly debated.

It's a fact

For anyone who would like support or further information relating to their sexuality, whether they think or know they are heterosexual, homosexual or bisexual, there are many help lines and websites they can visit (see page 47). They should also find out about safer sex messages, such as how to protect against STIs.

In the past

Several ancient cultures accepted and sometimes revered homosexuals. These included Ancient Greeks and Romans, Native American shamans in the Sac and Fox Nations tribes, samurais in Japan, and the Etoro people of Papua New Guinea. However, religions including Christianity and Islam decreed that homosexuality was against God's wishes (see chapter 3). As religion spread its influence globally, so did general acceptance that the Church could punish people, sometimes by death, for being homosexual. Homophobes blamed homosexuals at that time for many problems, including disease epidemics, for which they were burned at the stake to cleanse them of their so-called polluting influence on the world.

Against the law

In 1533, King Henry VIII of England made the first state law making sex between two men punishable, at that time by hanging. Henry used the law partly to take some power away from the Church. For example, he used spies to find evidence against nuns and monks and once they were found guilty, take monastery lands for the state. This law remained in place until 1861,

▼ Homosexuality was sufficiently acceptable in Ancient Rome for the Emperor Hadrian to have matching marble busts made of himself and his lover Antinous. However, Hadrian lived in a privileged sector of society and for most Romans, especially with the rise in Christianity towards the end of the Empire, homosexuality was not possible.

case study

Oscar Wilde

Oscar Wilde was a famous playwright and poet of the late nineteenth century. He was married to Constance Lloyd but as a homosexual had various affairs with men. After a very public friendship with Lord Alfred Douglas, Lloyd's angry father, the Marquis of Queensberry, accused Wilde of having sex with Douglas. Wilde took Queensberry to court to prove his innocence, but was convicted of earlier acts of indecency with other men. He spent 1895 to 1897 in Reading prison doing hard labour. His health suffered so much that he died just three years after his release.

A statue of Oscar Wilde in his native Dublin. ▶

when punishment was generally imprisonment, although the last execution for the crime in the UK was in 1837. As a result, for hundreds of years homosexual people kept their sexual orientation secret for fear of harassment and arrest by the police, public humiliation at trials, or losing their jobs if 'found out'.

Proving homosexuality

In Victorian times, people suspected of being homosexual were often examined by doctors to find proof, and this led the medical profession to search for scientific reasons for homosexuality. Some, for example, claimed that gay men had enlarged areas of their brains normally

bigger in women. Finding few physical explanations for homosexuality, Victorian doctors concluded it was a mental illness.

It's a fact

Many homosexuals in the twentieth century were sent to psychiatric hospitals for treatment, such as electric shock therapy and counselling. Homosexuality was classified as a mental illness until 1973 by the USA, the World Health Organisation until 1990, China until 2001 and India until 2009.

In 1969 the Stonewall Inn and the surrounding area were the site of a series of demonstrations and riots that led to the formation of the modern gay rights movement in the United States.

The struggle for gay rights

An early pioneer for gay rights was German lawyer Magnus Hirschfeld, who founded the Scientific-Humanitarian Committee that campaigned for changes to laws relating to homosexuality in Germany, the Netherlands and Austria in 1897. By the 1920s authorities allowed gay publications and nightclubs in large German cities. The rise of the violently intolerant Nazi regime in the 1930s closed them down and homosexuals were persecuted. For example, homosexuals were imprisoned, forced to wear pink triangles on their clothes, and many were beaten to death.

Following the struggle for freedom during World War II, European countries started to give more freedom to homosexual people. For example, in 1967 private meetings between gay men of 21 and over (and not in the military) were deemed no longer illegal.

Stonewall

Many people claim that the gay rights movement truly began in 1969 after the Stonewall Inn, a gay bar in New York, USA, was raided by police, sparking a riot lasting three nights. Hundreds of people fought and protested against being arrested for just having a good time in a club. The publicity triggered the formation of gay and lesbian political groups and encouraged many homosexual people to come out.

The gay rights movement spread and by the mid-1970s the first openly gay politicians were elected in the USA, including Nancy Wechsler and Harvey Milk. Gradually gay rights laws started to change. By 1980 it was illegal in the USA to discriminate against homosexuals based on their sexual orientation, but laws criminalizing gay sex remained in 12 North American states including Texas and Georgia up until 2003.

Harvey Milk's nephew, Stuart, accepts a Presidential Medal of Freedom on behalf of Harvey from President Obama. The medal is the highest civilian honour in the United States. President Obama praised Harvey Milk as someone who 'saw an imperfect world and set about improving it'.

Campaigns for change

The gay rights movement has had different political focuses at different times. For example, in the 1980s a major aim was to increase government funding for research into HIV/AIDS, then especially prevalent amongst the gay community. But one of the most important in the context of equal rights is same-sex marriage. Legal same-sex unions similar to marriage did happen occasionally in the past. For example, in mediaeval France, men could pledge to live together sharing bread, wine and money using 'affreremont' or brotherhood contracts. However, more widespread legal acceptance of same-sex unions has only started to happen in some countries at the end of the twentieth century.

viewpoints

'I can only hope that ...gay doctors will come out, the gay lawyers, the gay judges, gay bankers, gay architects ... I hope that every professional gay will say 'enough', come forward and tell everybody, wear a sign, let the world know. Maybe that will help.'
Harvey Milk, 1978

'If homosexuality was the normal way, God would have made Adam and Bruce.'
Anita Bryant, gay rights opponent, 1977

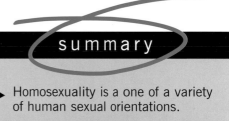

summary

▶ Homosexuality is a one of a variety of human sexual orientations.

▶ Acceptance of homosexual people depends largely on the religious and cultural views of individuals, groups and governments, and these have varied through time.

▶ Different places have different levels of acceptance and different laws about gay rights.

CHAPTER 2

Why get married?

Almost every culture in history has included some form of marriage and marriage was an essential part of the structure of those societies. It ensured partners in a marriage had rights and that their children would be cared for. It helped societies grow, because men traditionally worked while women cared for the home and children. It also ensured that when someone died their property would be inherited by their children and family. In fact Ancient Hebrew law required a man to marry his deceased brother's widow.

Different forms of marriage

Marriage between a man and a woman used to be more of a contract than a matter of love or choice. In most cultures, families or communities decided who married who. In the past and still in many cultures today, people may feel under pressure to marry someone from within their own tribe or group. In traditional societies, marriages are arranged by the couple's family. Partners may be chosen to bring social and economic advantages to their two families, although families also try to choose partners who are compatible with each other. In Western societies, young adults usually meet and choose their own partners.

Marriage today

Today some people choose to stay single and many others choose to live together without getting married. They believe that people do not need to get married to have a successful and long-lasting relationship in which they are committed to each other and their families.

A wedding couple taking their wedding vows in front of friends and family.

Given that if you are not religious there is no necessity for most people to get married, why do homosexual couples still want to tie the knot? Some people say they want the security and legal rights that marriage provides for themselves and for their children. Some want to declare their commitment to each other in front of friends, family and the wider community. They want to express their intention to stand together in good times and bad, through all the joys and challenges life brings. Many couples get married simply because they love each other and it feels right.

viewpoints

'Yes I do feel different, more respected by society – because having a ring on my finger shows that I am committed. ... If we are aping heterosexuals, so what? Declaring your love for someone is wonderful, having your loved ones there to witness it is even better.'
Shelley Duffy Silas, after marrying her partner, novelist Stella Silas Duffy in 2010

'I'm in a place right now where I don't want to get married. I don't think in this day and age you need to.'
Enrique Iglesias, singer (when asked whether he and tennis player Anna Kournikova were married)

▼ Same-sex couples say that getting married gives them a strong sense that they are in a long-term relationship, as it does for heterosexual couples.

▲ The rights of children in many cultures depend on whether their parents are married or not.

Legal aspects of marriage

Heterosexual couples have the benefit of many legal and economic benefits of marriage. However, no matter how long an unmarried couple's relationship has lasted, the law in most places still treats them as separate individuals if that relationship ends. For example, a married person automatically inherits their partner's money and property if that person dies. This is generally not the case for unmarried couples. After an unmarried relationship ends, neither partner has to provide financial support to the other. Unmarried couples may also miss out on tax credits, which are reductions in how much tax they pay the government, financial assistance if their partner is away on military service, medical treatment and other benefits.

Family rights

Unmarried couples are not entitled to other, more personal legal rights either. Legally, children of unmarried parents don't have the same basic rights as children of married couples when it comes to their parents. Neither the parent nor the child has visitation rights if the parents separate and if one parent dies, the second parent has no legal right to care for the child. There are other considerations too. If a couple is not married they would not automatically get 'next-of-kin' status and rights to visit and take important decisions about their partner's medical care in an emergency, even if they had been together for many years and the partner was estranged from the rest of his or her family. They would also be unable to choose how to dispose of their loved one's remains.

DIY documents

Opponents to same-sex marriage argue that same-sex couples, like heterosexual couples who do not marry, can make legal arrangements that give them many of the same rights as married couples. For example, couples can draw up legal documents that grant them child custody or plan how to divide joint property and money in case of a separation. Unmarried couples can also make wills so that if they die, their partner will inherit their home, money and pensions. However, these arrangements would not cover all the benefits afforded to other couples by their married status, such as next-of-kin status in times of emergency.

▼ In an emergency, only people who have next-of-kin status may be allowed at a patient's bedside.

case study

Banned from her partner's bedside

In February 2007, Janice Langbehn, her partner of 18 years Lisa Pond, and their three adopted children, aged 9, 11 and 13 were about to set off on a cruise from Florida when Ms Pond collapsed. Florida did not recognise same-sex partnerships so as Pond lay dying of a brain haemorrhage in hospital, Langbehn was fighting to see her. She said afterwards that she and their children were only allowed to see Pond briefly before she died 24 hours later.
'I have this deep sense of failure for not being at Lisa's bedside when she died,' Langbehn said. 'How I get over that I don't know, or if I ever do.'

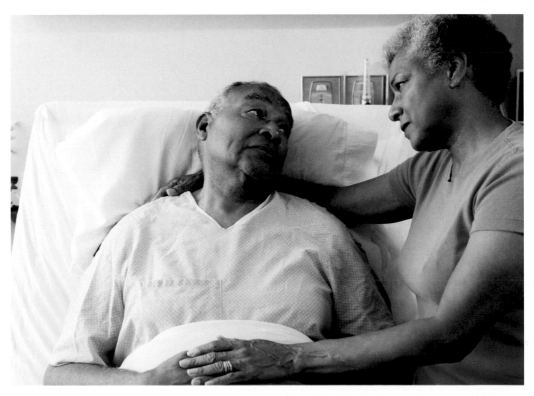

Civil unions and partnerships

In many countries same-sex unions are not allowed at all, but in some places, including the UK, New Zealand and Brazil, same-sex couples can register a formal commitment to one another in a domestic or civil partnership, also known as a civil union. This gives them legal recognition for their relationship and many of the same rights and responsibilities as married couples.

There are some differences, for example marriage ceremonies for opposite-sex couples can be either religious or civil, whereas a civil partnership can only be created by a civil ceremony. A partnership is formed when the couple signs papers and it doesn't have to be a public ceremony, whereas a marriage happens when the couple exchanges spoken words and signs the register. Denmark was the

first country to establish legal same-sex civil partnerships in 1989. It was soon followed by several other mostly Northern European countries during the 1990s.

▼ Two men signing the register at their Civil Partnership Ceremony, watched by the Registrar.

case study

Choosing marriage in Iceland

Iceland's Prime Minister, Johanna Sigurdardottir and her long-term partner, Jonina Leosdottir, took part in a civil union ceremony in 2002. It gave them the same rights and benefits as married heterosexual couples, but they still wanted to have a full 'marriage'. In June 2010 Iceland's parliament voted to make marriage a gender-neutral institution, that includes 'man and man' and 'woman and woman' in its definitions of marriage. This replaced the former system of registered partnerships and granted homosexual couples all the benefits and obligations of marriage, including adoption. Sigurdardottir and Leosdottir changed their civil union into a marriage on the very first day that the new law came into force.

Johanna Sigurdardottir was Iceland's, and the world's, first openly homosexual head of state. ▶

Civil unions vs. marriage

While many homosexual couples are satisfied with the option of a civil union or partnership, others feel aggrieved that they cannot have a marriage. One reason for this is that although a civil partnership gives homosexual couples most of same legal rights, it does not give all of them. There are often differences to do with the right to adopt children. For example, in Latin America same-sex civil unions are legal in Uruguay and some states in Brazil but these contracts do not give homosexual couples the right to adopt.

Some supporters of same-sex marriage also say that civil partnerships and unions do not have the same symbolic status as a marriage. They say that it is a second-class status and that civil unions should be replaced by gender-neutral marriage.

Same-sex unions in the USA

In the USA different states have different policies. In 1996 the US Congress brought in the Defense of Marriage Act, which prompted most US states to define marriage as purely heterosexual and to not recognise same-sex marriages from other states.

However, several states had different ideas. For example, California started to give licences for same-sex domestic partnerships, with equivalent legal rights as married heterosexual couples in 2003. In 2004 officials in San Francisco, a city in California with a high proportion of homosexual people in its population, started to issue same-sex marriage licences, but these were not recognised by other places in the same state! In early 2008 state judges ruled that it was illegal to limit marriage to a man and a woman, by late 2008 reversed its decision (see pages 4-5), and in 2013 was considering reversing it again, each time because of public pressure.

Around the world

More countries are gradually finding that there is no reason not to give homosexual people equal marriage rights. The first official same-sex marriage happened in 2001 in the Netherlands, and countries including Canada, Spain, South Africa and Argentina had changed their marriage laws by the end of 2012 (see box on page 19). In some places there are still different laws about marriage within a country. For example, civil unions are allowed in Mexico, but gay marriage, which gives homosexual couples extra rights such as adoption, is only legal in Mexico City. In 2013 both the UK and French governments proposed bills allowing same-sex marriage that awaited final ruling before passing into law.

▼ Children joining in a protest against a ruling by the Spanish parliament in 2005 to allow same-sex couples to marry and adopt children in Madrid. The banner reads 'Marriage = A man and a woman.'

In Mexico City in 2009 marriage was defined for the first time as a free union between two people, not just a man and a woman. In the rest of the country, same-sex marriage is recognised but not performed.

It's a fact

Same-sex marriage around the world

Place	Date legalised
Netherlands	2001
Belgium	2003
Massachusetts, USA	2004
Canada	2005
Spain	2005
South Africa	2006
Connecticut, USA	2008
Mexico City, Mexico	2009
Norway	2009
Sweden	2009
Iowa, Vermont, Maine and District of Columbia, USA	2009
Portugal	2010
Iceland	2010
Argentina	2010
New Hampshire, USA	2010
Washington, USA	2012
Denmark	2012

summary

► Marriage gives both partners in a couple legal rights and responsibilities to each other and their children.

► Most countries in the world do not offer marriage to homosexual couples.

► In some countries, homosexual couples can enter into a civil union or partnership which gives them most of the same rights and responsibilities as marriage.

19

CHAPTER 3

Religious rite or civil right?

In many countries the main obstacle to same-sex marriage is religious objection. Many religious leaders and followers object to homosexual marriage because they believe that their religion tells them homosexuality is sinful. They say that homosexuality is against the Christian Bible, the Muslim Qur'an and other holy books.

There are passages in sacred texts that condemn homosexual acts and negative passages about homosexuality in the scriptures and other holy books. For example, sentences like 'If a man lies with a man as one lies with a woman, both of them have done what is detestable. They must be put to death; their blood will be on their own heads.' from the Bible (Leviticus 20:13) lead to the Catholic Church's tough stance on homosexuality and its call for homosexual Catholics to live chaste lives.

Religious interpretations

As with most debates on ethical issues, one of the main problems for religious leaders is how religious books should be interpreted. In modern society religious people do many things that are supposedly forbidden by their holy texts. For example, the Bible tells Christians they should not wear mixed fibres, eat shellfish or let disabled people into temples, but none of these edicts is followed to the letter. And there are passages in the Bible that some

▼ The Pope is the leader of the Catholic Church, which teaches that while homosexuality is not sinful, homosexual acts are. However, there are ordinary Catholics who do not agree with this edict.

Archbishop Desmond Tutu, who retired from public service in 2010, tirelessly campaigned for equal rights not only for black people, but also for homosexual people in South Africa and worldwide.

interpret as showing same-sex unions as normal, '... Jonathan became one in spirit with David and he loved him as himself.' In fact, many people do not believe they have to take every word of their holy text literally in order to be a follower of their particular faith. They say that texts written long ago were written for that particular time and were never intended to be taken literally and believe that such texts are open to interpretation because they were meant to offer guidance only.

Range of opinions

Within every religious movement there is a great range of opinion. Some Christians condemn homosexuality but many others accept it, regarding homosexuality as a sexual orientation which is normal and natural for some adults. Many religious leaders welcome homosexuals to their religious communities. For example, the Anglican communities in North America,

Europe, Australia, New Zealand and southern Africa generally do not regard homosexuality as sinful. However, in the majority of Africa and the West Indies, and in other places where there are evangelical Anglican groups, Anglicans believe that homosexuality should be condemned.

viewpoints

'Everyone is an insider, there are no outsiders – whatever their beliefs, whatever their colour, gender or sexuality.'
Archbishop Desmond Tutu, 2004

'Transsexuals and homosexuals will never enter the kingdom of heaven and it is not me who says this, but Saint Paul. ... It may not be their fault, but acting against nature and the dignity of the human body is an insult to God.'
Leading Roman Catholic Cardinal Javier Lozano Barragán, 2009

▲ A traditional religious view of marriage is one that promotes the idea of the nuclear family – a family with two parents, one male and one female, and their children. Today many families do not fit this model.

The meaning of marriage

While many religious people accept homosexuals into their communities, they draw the line at allowing same-sex marriages or unions. The reason traditionally given for this, for example by the Catholic Church, is that marriage is for procreation, to create and care for children. Unlike the offspring of most other species of animals in the world, children need to be looked after for a long time before they are ready to look after themselves. Traditionally marriage provided a way of helping parents fulfill their duties and responsibilities to their children. The argument of many religions is that since same-sex couples cannot produce children, same-sex marriage should not be permitted.

Modern marriage

Supporters of same-sex marriage say that marriage today is not simply about having children. Since the 1960s and the advent of new forms of contraception such as the Pill, couples have been able to choose not to have children, although some Catholic couples follow decrees from Catholic leaders in Rome saying that artificial contraception should not be used. The marriages of heterosexual couples who choose not to or are unable to have children are still considered valid. The idea of natural law, where only a man and a woman can have a child, has also been challenged by medical developments to help childless couples have children, such as donor insemination and surrogacy.

A religious rite

Another argument that some religious opponents to same-sex unions give is that marriage is a religious rite and that the word 'marriage' should only be used in the context of religion. In Islam, for example, marriage is considered to be gift from God or a kind of service to God, and in Judaism marriage is believed to have been introduced by God. Even in countries where civil partnerships are offered, most ceremonies have had to be

secular, or non-religious. Religious aspects of heterosexual weddings, such as hymns or Bible readings, are not allowed in most civil partnerships in order to preserve the definition of religious marriage as the union of a man and a woman.

viewpoints

'Marriage is holy, while homosexual acts go against the natural moral law. Homosexual acts 'close the sexual act to the gift of life. ... Under no circumstances can they be approved.'
Statement from the Vatican, the centre of the Catholic faith

'Religions are not immune to a basic law of history: Everything changes. Over time, some faiths become more conservative, others more liberal.'
Ron Grossman, journalist

For most Catholics, marriage is a religious rite reserved for a man and a woman only and intended for procreation, or the production of children.

▲ Richard and Mildred Loving's wedding in 1958 led to their arrest and eventually to a change in law in 1967 to allow inter-racial marriage in the USA.

Is marriage a civil right?

Many supporters of same-sex marriage say that marriage is not so much a religious as a civil rights issue. Civil rights are the rights of individuals not to be discriminated against in areas of their life, such as employment, voting in elections etc. In ethical debates about same-sex marriage supporters say that laws prohibiting any type of same-sex marriage are discriminatory. They are against an individual's civil rights and no different to laws in the past that prevented inter-racial couples from marrying. These laws have been overturned, for example in the USA in 1967, and today many people believe that it is just a matter of time before laws preventing same-sex couples from marrying are overturned too.

In South Africa for example, people fought long and hard to end apartheid, the system of discrimination whereby white people had many more rights than other people, especially black people. After the apartheid regime was toppled in 1990 the new constitution in South Africa made discrimination illegal and there was a clause in the constitution that also made discrimination based on sexual identity illegal. In 2006 South Africa amended its marriage laws to include same-sex unions.

Same-sex marriage and discrimination

Some opponents of same-sex marriage claim that gay rights cannot be equated with racial equality because while people do not choose their ethnicity, they say that people choose to be homosexual and that a chosen behaviour does not deserve special legal protection. Supporters of same-sex marriage say that homosexuals no more choose their sexual orientation than they choose their gender or their ethnicity; it is simply who they are. And if this is the case, to discriminate against someone because of their homosexuality is the same as any other form of discrimination, including sexism and racism. They believe that just as inter-racial marriage is no longer regarded as a subject for ethical debate for most people, the same will be true of same-sex marriage in the future.

▼ A same-sex couple is married in the chapel of Robben Island Museum, which was once the prison where Nelson Mandela and other black civil rights protestors were held by the South African government during the second half of the twentieth century.

Legal systems have religious roots

Legal systems in many countries have religious roots and religion has had a strong influence on marriage laws in particular. For example the legal system in the USA evolved out of the laws contained in the Bible and religious texts are the basis for Islamic and Jewish family law. Some people believe that this gives religious authorities the right to influence law-makers in order to prevent same-sex marriage today. They say that if religious freedom is a legal right, then it is their belief that it goes against the religious freedom of the majority to have to recognise a relationship that those people consider sinful.

Testing Europe on gay marriage

In June 2010 Horst Michael Schalk and Johann Franz Kopf took their case to the European Court of Human Rights. They argued by not allowing them the right to marry, their home country of Austria was violating their right to be free from discrimination and to privacy and family life, as guaranteed by the European Convention on Human Rights.

In 2010 Austria was one of the 40 member nations of the Council of Europe that did not allow same-sex marriage; the other seven member nations already allowed it. If the Court had agreed that Austria was violating Schalk and Kopf's rights, the people of other member states such as Russia, Italy, or Poland would also have been able to successfully challenge the ban on same-sex marriage in their countries. The Court felt this meant they were voting to effectively force member states to legalise same-sex marriage and Shalk and Kopf lost their case. However, the vote was close and supporters believe it was a test case that will lead to full equality for same-sex families in future.

▼ Horst Michael Schalk on the right discusses his complaint against Austria with his legal counsellor at the European Court of Human Rights in Strasbourg, France.

▲ Opponents of same-sex marriage outside the State House in Boston, Massachusetts, USA in January 2007 where judges were voting to decide whether the issue of laws banning gay marriage should be put to a people's vote, or referendum. The eventual vote was 151 votes opposed to the proposed referendum against 45 in favour.

Marriage as a legal contract

Supporters of same-sex marriage counter such arguments by saying that laws preventing homosexual marriage derive from religious texts and have no place in a country where the laws are secular (non-religious). In the USA, for example, the constitution is based on the principle of separation of church and state and this is an integral part of American government. If marriage by the state is a secular activity and a legal contract, the government cannot keep or make laws just because a religion says it should.

They say that allowing marriage rights to same-sex couples would not force religious leaders to perform these ceremonies or hold them in their places of worship. People of faith would be free to have different views on those marriages to the government, as they do already. For example, the US government recognises the second marriages of all previously divorced couples and gives them the same rights as every other married couple. On the other hand, the Catholic Church is free to rule that it considers second marriages invalid because it does not sanction divorce.

People of faith

The idea of same-sex marriages and civil unions falling under the category of state-sanctioned partnerships has implications for homosexual couples of faith. What do same-sex Hindu, Sikh, Jewish, Muslim or Christian couples do if they want to marry in their place of worship and according to the principles of their faith?

Some religious communities who do not wish to offer same-sex marriages to their congregations fear that changes in laws offering civil unions or partnerships will one day force them to do so. In 2013 MPs in the UK voted to pass a bill enabling same-sex couples to get married in religious ceremonies in England and Wales. They said the change would not be forced

◄ Rev Alicia Heath-Toby stands next to her partner Saundra Toby-Heath (right) at the Liberation in Truth Unity Fellowship Church, where she is pastor in New Jersey, USA. In New Jersey homosexual couples cannot marry in their places of worship.

on religious organisations and the bill specifies that the Church of England and Church in Wales would be banned from offering same-sex marraiges. The legal ban may have the effect of protecting the Church of England from legal claims that it is bound to marry anyone who requests it. However, many traditionalists in the UK and elsewhere still fear that changes in laws like this might lead to all churches being forced to allow gay weddings. Their argument is that when same-sex marriages are allowed in places of worship by law, they might face legal challenges by couples who take them to court under anti-discrimination laws.

Religious support for same-sex marriage

In some countries, there are religious leaders who have conducted their own wedding ceremonies for homosexual couples, or offer blessings after a civil union. British Quakers have been celebrating same-sex unions through special acts of worship since 1987 and a

Quaker same-sex commitment follows a similar format to a Quaker wedding with the couple exchanging vows within their worshipping community. In 2005 in the USA the Episcopal Church and the Evangelical Lutheran Church started to celebrate same-sex marriages in church. In the same year the United Church of Christ, which has 1.3 million followers, became the largest Christian Church in the United States to support and offer same-sex marriage.

viewpoints

'I really wasn't comfortable with the idea of going to a civil registrar: it's not what marriage is about for us. It's a solemn and binding commitment in the presence of God. Without some recognition of that religious element, it certainly put me off the idea of getting married.'

Chris Campbell, a UK Quaker in a long-term homosexual relationship with a Roman Catholic

'It is a step towards forcing churches to conduct same-sex unions that would go against their beliefs. Changing the law will further blur the distinction between marriage and what the Government put forward as a purely secular ceremony.'

Andrea Williams of the Christian Legal Centre speaking of the UK government lifting the ban on religious premises holding same-sex partnerships

It's a fact

The Quakers – or Religious Society of Friends – view marriage as the Lord's work and not that of priests or magistrates. They believe that religious ceremonies should recognise committed relationships regardless of the genders involved. In their book on Quaker faith 'same-sex marriages can be prepared, celebrated, witnessed, recorded and reported to the State, as opposite-sex marriages are.' The Quakers have formally acknowledged same-sex relationships since the 1960s and are the first religious group in the UK to approve marriages for homosexuals.

summary

▶ Some religions teach that marriage should only happen between a man and a woman.

▶ Some people believe that same-sex marriage is a civil right.

▶ Some religions carry out same-sex marriages or blessings after a civil union for followers in their places of worship.

Families and children

It is possible for same-sex couples to have children in several different ways. Some couples have children from a previous heterosexual relationship and some adopt children whose parents cannot bring them up. Lesbian couples can have children through donor insemination, which uses sperm from a donor to help one of the women in the couple to become pregnant. Surrogacy is when another woman carries and gives birth to a baby for a couple who want to have a child, using donated eggs and sperm. Co-parenting is when, for example, a lesbian woman and a homosexual man combine their eggs and sperm (usually using an insemination kit) to parent a child.

It's a fact

Barrie and Tony Drewitt-Barlow, of Danbury, Essex, hit the headlines in 1999 when their twin daughters Aspen and Saffron, were born to a surrogate mother in California and became the first British children to be registered as having two fathers and no mother.

Legal issues

The laws about same-sex couples having children vary around the world. For example, Portugal passed a law to legalise same-sex marriage in 2010, but rejected

▼ Noah, 22 months, and Mackenlie, 9, pose with their parents, Hazel (left) and Donna Jensen-Wysinger in Salt Lake City, USA. Hazel is the biological parent of Noah, and Donna is the biological parent of Mackenlie, and the two lesbians cross-adopted each other's child to legally form their family.

proposals to allow homosexual couples to adopt. In the USA, surrogacy for same-sex couples is legal in some states, while in others it is considered a criminal act. Some same-sex couples who are banned from adopting or using surrogates in their own country, go elsewhere to become parents.

In the case of co-parenting the couple may choose to legally agree some issues before the baby is born, such as how much time the child will spend with each parent and how much will each partner pay for the child's upbringing, in case of disagreements later.

case study

Israeli parents bring baby home from India

Israel doesn't allow same-sex parents to legally adopt a baby or use the services of a surrogate mother so Yonatan and Omer Gher started their family in India. Although India criminalises homosexuality, it does allow same-sex couples to hire a surrogate mother to deliver their child there. So, after a long search, Yonatan and Omer found a suitable surrogate in Mumbai and their son Evyatar was conceived using sperm from Yonatan and eggs from an anonymous donor in a fertility clinic.

They returned to Israel during the pregnancy but kept in touch with the mother by email and returned to India in time for their son's birth. Before they could take him home, the Israeli government required the new parents to do a DNA test to prove their paternity. Back in Israel, the walls of the couple's home are covered in pictures of their baby boy and they do shifts to take care of him round the clock. They hope to return to Mumbai and use the same donor to have a brother or sister for Evyatar.

Omer Gher and Yonatan chose their son's name – Evyatar – from the Bible. It means 'more fathers' in Hebrew.

The ethical debates around same-sex parenting get to the heart of what being a family really means and what it is that children most need from any parents or carers.

viewpoints

'It was normal to me, it was all I knew. I remember one day in school a guy came in and said 'your parents are lesbians'. But before that I'd never put a word to it. I went home and said to my mothers 'are you lesbians?' I think I was eight or nine.'

Evan Barry, a 23-year-old from Dublin who has two mothers

'A baby is not a trophy – the child's welfare has to be considered. These children are more likely to experiment with same-sex relationships. They're more likely to be confused and hurt.'

Dale O'Leary, author of *One Man, One Woman: A Catholic's Guide to Defending Marriage*

Mums or dads?

Opponents of same-sex families think that children need one parent of each sex to develop properly and that the traditional ideal of a nuclear family should be followed as closely as possible. They believe that children need both male and female influences and if a child's natural parents are unable to look after them, the child should only be adopted into a family where there are both mother and father figures. Some think that while homosexual relationships should be accepted, the law should encourage the ideal of the nuclear family by making it illegal for same-sex couples to have families by adoption or other means.

For many other people, the sex of a child's parents is not the issue. The real issue for them is whether those parents will nurture and love the child and give it the stability it needs, and both men and women are

It's a fact

There are about 600,000 same-sex couples living in the USA. Two-fifths of same-sex couples in the USA aged 22 to 55 are raising children. In total they are raising more than 250,000 children under the age of 18.

equally capable of this. They say that society is changing and the traditional model of the nuclear family with a married mother and father is no longer the only acceptable alternative. There are many different kinds of families around us, including single-parent families, step-families and those in which children are brought up by their grandparents. In a world where there is a shortage of foster parents and there are many children waiting for adoption, many people ask why shouldn't homosexual couples be able to offer these children the stable and loving home they need?

Gay parents, gay kids?

Another issue in this debate is to do with sexuality. Some people think that children of same-sex couples are significantly more likely to be homosexual themselves. They argue that, if a child's main role models are his or her parents, growing up in a same-sex family will give the child a one-sided view of sexual orientation. However, most of the world's homosexual men and women have heterosexual parents, and according to the American Psychological Association, numerous research studies have shown that children from same-sex households describe themselves as heterosexual in roughly the same proportion as from more conventional families. Most scientists agree that some babies seem to be simply born with a predisposition to homosexuality.

▼ Whether a family interacts successfully and is happy and fulfilled depends on the mutual understanding and respect of individuals within it, regardless of their gender or sexual orientation.

Stress and stigma?

Some people say that same-sex couples should not become parents because of the bullying and problems that their children can face. Homophobic language and behaviour are still common in many places and when a gay couple has a child, that child can become a victim of this prejudice too. As much as they love their families, some young people may keep quiet about their same-sex parents to avoid bullying or they might find it difficult having them come to school for parent-teacher meetings or sports days. Some young people could feel isolated and threatened by other people's abusive attitudes and behaviour towards their parents' homosexuality.

Attitudes and acceptance

There are people who do not accept that same-sex parents can offer children a happy, stable home. Some same-sex couples believe that by living in a place as a successful same-sex family, they can help to overcome such prejudice. Others choose to live in places that are more accepting. For example, cities tend to be more diverse than rural areas and more respectful of non-traditional families.

Some children who have been teased or bullied about having same-sex parents say that they have learned to be more empathetic and accepting of people who are different because they know how it feels to be unfairly judged. For some, it increases their respect for their parents who have been brave enough to be true to their sexuality in the face of criticism. What matters is whether or not their parents have always been there for them, not their parents' sexual orientation.

▼ Bullies often attack things they don't understand or that they perceive as 'different' and as having same-sex parents is something many people are unfamiliar with some children of same-sex families face bullying at school.

Growing up with two mums

Jeff DeGroot is a young adult who was raised by two lesbian mothers in Oregon, USA. He never felt he missed out on having a father and his parents did all the things people might expect a father to do, like playing baseball with him and taking him hiking. His mothers, Elisabeth and Meg, always made sure that he had several male role models in his life so that no one could suggest he was missing out on anything by not having a dad.

He had fun deciding what to call his parents: 'If I'm on one side of the house and I want to talk to my biological mom, I'll yell, "Mother." If Meg says, "Yes?" I'll say, "No, other mother"!'

Jeff grew up in Corvallis, Oregon, a college town in a liberal US state, in a time and place where same-sex couples were generally more accepted and he did not have a problem with teasing or bullying from his classmates or community. In fact some of Jeff's friends thought he was cool for having two lesbian mums and would say, 'Oh, you got two moms? I gotta meet them!'

What upsets one of his mothers, Elisabeth, most, is critics who say that children of same-sex couples will grow up physiologically damaged. 'That makes me mad. I know better. There's Jeff,' she says.

▲ Maureen Kilian smiles as Cindy Meneghin asks her to marry her as her son Josh looks on. The New Jersey couple were celebrating a Supreme Court ruling that homosexuals are entitled to the same rights as heterosexuals.

summary

▶ Same-sex couples can have children in several different ways, for example by adoption, artificial insemination, surrogacy and co-parenting.

▶ Different countries around the world have different laws regarding adoption, surrogacy and other methods of same-sex parenting.

▶ Many studies show that there is no real difference between children of same-sex couples and heterosexual couples.

CHAPTER 5

Effects on society

Another debate that centres on homosexual marriage is how it will affect the structures of society and everyday life. Will same-sex marriage, as some fear, change the status and expectations of marriage and bring an increase in divorce rates and fractured families? Or will it, as others believe, serve to strengthen the institution of marriage and bring a range of benefits to individuals and communities?

A slippery slope…

Some opponents of same-sex marriage fear that if countries allow it, marriage could be transformed into a variety of relationship contracts between two, three, or more

◄ Barrie and Tony Drewitt-Barlow (front and back left) at the church baptism of their son Orlando and twins Jasper and Dallas in 2010, attended also by the children's surrogate mothers. Many people believe that public acceptance of same-sex couples' commitment to union and to their unusual family set-ups might be improved by allowing more same-sex marriages.

people of the same or different sexes. They say that without a firm definition of marriage, options might become endless and that these non-traditional families could break down the family values upon which society is built. Many people question this logic. They point to the fact that, in some cultures, including the Mormons of the USA, polygamous marriages have been around for centuries, well before any same-sex marriages, but remain a minority choice.

Divorce

Another criticism of same-sex marriage is that it could increase the rates of divorce. Organizations such as the US-based Family Research Council (FRC), which opposes same-sex marriage, claim that same-sex couples divorce sooner than heterosexual couples. To support this, they present official data on marriage from across the USA, involving tens of thousands of heterosexual people, showing that around 70 per cent stay married for 10 or more years. They contrast this with a Gay/Lesbian Consumer Online Census of under 8,000 people from 2003/2004 showing that most homosexual relationships last less than three years.

The conclusion they draw from this is that homosexual partners in a same-sex marriage would not insist on sexual fidelity and that by having affairs outside marriage, this would lessen the idea of marriage as a long-term commitment and make it more likely that heterosexual couples would be unfaithful too, leading to more divorces.

People supporting same-sex marriage say this evidence does not prove same-sex marriage leads to more divorce. They argue that data used by the FRC are not

comparable as they contrast government statistics with online answers from a small questionnaire, and say that they also prove nothing. For example, they cite the fact that, since same-sex marriage became legal in 2004, divorce rates in Massachusetts have remained some of the lowest in the USA. They point out that overall divorce rates are increasing in many countries that do not allow same-sex marriage, because this reflects other changes in society.

It's a fact

Divorce rate statistics should be read with caution. In the USA around 50 per cent of all marriages end in divorce, but in India the figure is around 1 per cent. This does not mean that Indians are more likely to be happily married, but that divorce is less acceptable culturally than in the USA. The divorce rate is falling in countries such as the UK. This is partly a consequence of people getting married when they are older and more committed to each other, but partly because fewer people overall are getting married.

viewpoints

'Americans will see that when lesbians and gay men are given access to most of the rights and obligations of civil marriage, the sky will not fall and the institution of marriage will be even stronger.'
Evan Wolfson, American gay rights lawyer

'Homosexuals are not monogamous. They want to destroy the institution of marriage. It [same-sex marriage] will destroy marriage. It will destroy the Earth.'
Dr James Dobson, from Focus on the Family

Society stability

Some people believe that more widespread same-sex marriage could enhance the stability of society that others feel is at risk. If more homosexual people were allowed to marry, this could discourage promiscuity, and encourage stable relationships and the strong family values that conservatives want. Allowing married same-sex couples to adopt could help society by taking more children from care into stable family settings. UK statistics from 2010 suggest that three-quarters of children who are still in care by their sixteenth birthday will have a criminal conviction in the future.

A dangerous lifestyle?

There are concerns amongst some that same-sex marriage could expose more people to a homosexual lifestyle that they consider to be dangerous. Their reasoning is that by making same-sex marriage as acceptable as heterosexual marriage, homosexuality will become more widespread. Their argument rests on the notion that some homosexual people behave in ways that can endanger their own health and the health of others, such as having unprotected sex with several partners and thus risking the spread of diseases such as hepatitis and HIV/AIDS. HIV/AIDS is the world's most deadly infectious disease and the fourth biggest killer worldwide.

It is widely accepted that some homosexual people have higher rates of depression, suicide risk and lower life expectancy than most heterosexual people. Research has shown that the trauma of experiencing homophobic bullying is a significant cause of these statistics (see page 7).

A poster in Niger warns of the dangers of AIDS (SIDA). It stresses that the disease can be spread by heterosexuals and that condoms, abstinence from sex, and fidelity (having fewer partners) can help protect against AIDS.

Other people disagree with the idea that same-sex marriage will increase risky homosexual behaviour. They argue that potentially health-damaging promiscuous behaviour exists in heterosexuals too and that heterosexual AIDS/HIV affects millions of heterosexuals in addition to homosexuals. They suggest that, if people think homosexuals are more likely to be promiscuous, this could be an argument in favour of gay marriage, to encourage stability in relationships. Psychological problems such as depression are always more likely in people who are feel outside the mainstream society and face prejudice and homophobia, something which might be improved if same-sex marriage became more mainstream.

case study

Changing sex for society's sake in Iran

Iran's society is based in Islam and in general the country is very traditional in its view of gender – people should be either male or female heterosexuals. Homophobia is common. For example, in 2008 Iranian religious cleric Hojatol Kariminia said: 'Homosexuals are doing something unnatural and against religion. It is clearly stated in our Islamic law that such behaviour is not allowed because it disrupts the social order.'

People found guilty of having sex with someone of their own gender face public beating and sometimes execution. Perhaps surprisingly, transgender people – those who believe their true sexuality is opposite to the gender they were born with – are tolerated by the Iranian state. If officially diagnosed as transgender, people receive government support to have sex-changing surgery that transforms them physically into the opposite gender. Then their gender is changed on their birth certificate and they can even get married legally. The state considers this type of gender change much more acceptable and better for society than homosexuality.

◀ Maryam Khatoon Molkara (left, with her husband Mohammed) is a transgender woman who, in the 1980s, was the first Iranian man to have an officially approved sex-change operation. Now she runs a centre in Tehran which aims to help transsexuals in Iran and the region.

▲ Wedding receptions can be phenomenally expensive, lavish occasions that provide work for many people. Same-sex marriages and civil unions are a relatively new and affluent market targeted by the wedding industry worldwide.

Making money from same-sex marriage

Same-sex marriages generate money in different ways for any society. In places such as the UK or USA, the shared household income of married people is used to find out how much state help the government should give them. For example, the government might provide healthcare benefits to individuals but not to married couples because they can partly support each other financially. By allowing same-sex marriages, governments can save money on benefits. In 2003, a study estimated that New Jersey could save US$61 million each year by upgrading same-sex unions from domestic partnerships to marriages.

Same-sex marriage also brings money to places through the wedding industry. This includes the businesses that make a wedding happen, from jewellery and dress shops, to caterers, hotels and photographers. The average cost of a wedding is around £15,000 or US$21,000 in the UK or USA, not including a honeymoon and the income from a

same-sex marriage is often greater than its heterosexual equivalent. The average disposable income of homosexual people is higher than that of heterosexual people because typically they do not have families to spend money on. Many people refer to this money as the pink pound or dollar.

Chasing the pink pound

Researchers in 2008 estimated that, for California, legalising same-sex marriages could bring an extra US$700 million to the wedding industry and also US$65 million in marriage fees to the state government within three years. This was never tested as the state changed its mind over legalisation (see page 5). However, in the District of

It's a fact

Individuals in same-sex couples contribute to the United States economy: 71 per cent of them are employed compared with 65 per cent of individuals in married couples.

Pink Mountain tour company in Nepal offers same-sex weddings at the base of Mount Everest as part of Nepal's drive to welcome and make money from homosexual tourists.

case study

Gay tourism in Nepal

Homosexuality is not well tolerated in Asia in general, but Nepal plans to become a regional leader in tourism specifically aimed at homosexual people. Tourism is the biggest industry in Nepal yet has been severely affected both by the global economic crisis and also by civil war.

Although Nepal only made homosexuality legal in 2007, its government is considering legalising same-sex weddings. Sunil Pant is a homosexual member of Nepal's parliament who has fought for gay rights in Nepal. He has also set up a specialist travel agency for homosexual tourists called Pink Mountain that offers gay weddings and honeymoon trips in the country. The first unofficial lesbian wedding took place in June 2011 between two American women.

Columbia, revenue from same-sex marriages following legalisation there turned out to be much lower than expected. There are several reasons for this, such as the global economic crisis and the fact that for some same-sex couples, marriage is merely a legal formality of a union that has already have been celebrated. Nevertheless, in some places worldwide wedding planners and tourism authorities are trying to encourage same-sex weddings in the hope of a bigger share of the pink pound or dollar.

summary

▶ There is a debate over the impact of same-sex marriage on divorce rates, the stability of society and the incidence of dangerous homosexual behaviour.

▶ Same-sex marriage can bring social benefits such as legally adopting children in care and economic benefits for the wedding industry.

CHAPTER 6

Into the future

Are there too many cultural and religious obstacles to same-sex marriage in some places for it to ever become legal? Is the idea of equal rights for same-sex couples now sufficiently established that same-sex marriage will become the norm worldwide? Predicting the future of this debate is very tricky given the wide acceptance gap between different people and countries.

Almost there?

The histories of controversial topics, such as the abolition of slavery and winning equal rights for women, show that some laws and institutions take a long time to change. They often change in one place following key events in another. For example, Stonewall (see page 10) triggered a change in gay rights in the USA and worldwide.

Many people feel that same-sex marriage could soon be legalised across European countries, especially since the 2010 case at the European Court of Human Rights (see page 26) dismissed only narrowly a gay couple's claim that Austria took away their human rights by not letting them marry.

The desire for a change in homosexual equality was already there before the Stonewall riot, but it is commemorated today because it was the start of public awareness of this issue.

Other people question whether attitudes have really changed. Across US states the public consistently votes against same-sex marriage even in places where courts have made it legal, based on interpretations of the American constitution. In Texas the Board of Education plans to revise school textbooks based on the political views of the state's ruling Republican Party. In their 2010 Platform document, the party said that 'Homosexuality must not be presented as an acceptable "alternative" lifestyle in our public education and policy, nor should "family" be redefined to include homosexual "couples."'

At least there is debate about same-sex marriage in the USA, which is not the case in other parts of the world. For example, in Kenya in 2010 rumours of a possible gay wedding in the town of Mtwapa began a wave of homophobic violence which was condoned by the government.

▼ In 2010 human rights protestors worldwide, including here in South Africa, criticised Malawi's decision to sentence a same-sex couple to 14 years hard labour.

case study

Predicting the US future

In 2009, Nate Silver, a data analyst in the USA, predicted when different states would legalise same-sex marriage in the future. He looked at the percentage of people voting to ban same-sex marriage in the most recent poll in each state and the proportion of people who said religion was important in their day-to-day lives. He then assumed that each year there will be 2 per cent fewer voters who want to ban same-sex marriage, based on the trend in US states that have now legalised same-sex marriage.

He also predicted that the last ten states to drop the marriage ban would all be in the conservative south of the country (including Kentucky, Alabama and Mississippi) between 2019 and 2024. In 2012 Silver had to revise his figures because of new polls revealing that a majority of Americans favoured same-sex marriage. He thinks this means that same-sex marriage will spread faster through the states now.

Transforming society

The world is changing fast in many ways. At the start of the twentieth century black people, women and people with disabilities lived as second-class citizens with few or no voting rights and restricted freedom. At that time homosexuality was still almost universally illegal. A lot has changed since then, but it was not until the 1990s that same-sex unions were first legalised in some parts of the world. The concept of marriage has been rapidly changing. The world has moved on from a situation when marriages between people of different races were unacceptable, through acceptance of divorce, to same-sex marriage. Our ideas of what makes a family now include not only a man, a woman and their children, but also homosexual and transgender parents, test-tube babies, and children born from surrogate mothers.

case study

Argentina moves forward

At 4.05 am on 15 July 2010, hundreds of people waiting in the cold outside Argentina's Congress building in Buenos Aires heard that the Senate had approved same-sex marriage by 33 votes to 27. The law confirmed Argentina as a leader in gay rights in South America, despite strong opposition from the Roman Catholic Church. The evening before the vote, 60,000 people took part
in a march on Congress, organised by the Church, carrying orange flags symbolising opposition to the bill. Argentinians have religious freedom but Catholicism is the official religion and this has an impact on laws in the country, such as making abortion illegal. For many Argentinians the vote in favour of same-sex marriage is proof that the country is moving forward. Cesar Cigliutti, president of the Argentine Homosexual Community, said: "This is encouraging not just for our couples, but also because it is Argentine society valuing diversity."

▼ The banner held by supporters of same-sex marriage in Argentina reads 'The same love, the same rights, with the same name'.

▲ In March 2010, ten same-sex couples were married in the same ceremony in Washington DC, USA, after the nation's capital became the sixth place in the nation to recognise same-sex marriage.

The reason that same-sex marriage is being debated at all is that the leaders around the world increasingly value human rights, even when these are at odds with traditional cultural and religious views. It is every individual's right in a place to have the same rights as others, including the right to express his or her own beliefs, to achieve happiness, health and stability, and to get married. More and more people each year believe that a person's sexual orientation should not affect this.

It's a fact

Webster's Dictionary, 1913 on marriage: "The act of marrying, or the state of being married; legal union of a man and a woman for life, as husband and wife; wedlock; matrimony."

Merriam-Webster Dictionary, online edition, 2003: "(1) The state of being united to a person of the opposite sex as husband or wife in a consensual and contractual relationship recognized by law; (2) the state of being united to a person of the same sex in a relationship like that of a traditional marriage."

Glossary

Anglican Member of the Church of England, part of the Christian church.

Annul State officially that something is not valid any more.

Apartheid Political system in South Africa from 1948 and 1994 in which black people had fewer civil rights than white people and had to live apart and use separate buses, schools and restaurants.

Chaste State of not having sex with anyone or only with the person you are married to.

Civil partnership/union Same-sex relationship recognised by the government of a country or region to have equal legal status as the marriage between a man and woman.

Contraception Ways of preventing a woman from becoming pregnant including the use of condoms or pills. Contraception is sometimes called birth control.

Co-parenting When parents are not married, living together or in a sexual relationship but share the responsibility of raising children.

Custody Legal right or duty to take care of a child.

Donor insemination When a man agrees to give sperm to be inserted by doctors into the womb of a woman, hopefully to make her pregnant.

Evangelical Persuading others that Christian beliefs are the most important beliefs and that they should take on the Christian faith.

Hepatitis Disease of the liver caused by eating infected food or having contact with infected blood.

HIV/AIDS HIV is a virus that weakens the human immune system and AIDS is a range of symptoms often resulting in death that can result from HIV infection.

Inter-racial Between two races, sometimes used to describe relationships between black and white people.

Legal system Way of interpreting and enforcing laws distinctive to a particular country, region or place.

Natural law Basic principle that governs interactions between people, such as respect and fairness.

Next-of-kin status Legal authorisation of being closely related to or responsible for someone else. Next-of-kin can take part in decisions about the person, such as whether they should have medical treatment or where they should live.

Nuclear family Consisting of mother, father and children and considered a basic unit making up societies.

Persecute Treat others cruelly or unfairly, often based on race, sexual orientation or political views.

Pink pound/dollar Describes the wealth of or business resulting from the homosexual community.

Plaintiff Person making a formal complaint against something or someone in a law court.

Sacred text Writings considered holy as they are connected with God, and that are significant for religious people.

Sanction Give official permission for something to happen.

Secular Unconnected with religious or spiritual matters.

Self-harm Deliberately cut or otherwise injure yourself as a result of having emotional or mental difficulties.

Sexual orientation Whether you are homosexual, heterosexual or bisexual.

Shaman A spiritual and physical healer in some societies.

STI Sexually transmitted infection such as HIV or syphilis.

Surrogacy When a woman gives birth to a baby for another person who cannot have children.

Visitation rights Official legal permission for a parent (or grandparent) to visit a child (grandchild) they normally don't look after, for example following divorce, separation or death of its parents.

Timeline

1967   US Supreme Court strikes down a Virginia law against inter-racial marriage in the case of Richard and Mildred Loving.

Private meetings between gay adults becomes legal in the UK.

1969   Stonewall riots in New York spark the gay rights movement.

1970   Jack Baker and Jim McConnell unsuccessfully apply for a wedding licence in Minnesota, USA.

1973   American Psychiatric Association rules that homosexuality cannot be classified as a mental illness.

1980   Discrimination against homosexuals becomes illegal in the USA.

1987   Mock mass same-sex wedding takes place in Washington to highlight the tax benefits that same-sex couples are denied.

1989   Denmark becomes the first country to legalise same-sex partnerships.

2000   Vermont legalises first same-sex unions in the USA.

2001   Germany's and the Netherlands' first gay weddings take place.

2003   Parts of Canada and Massachusetts, USA, legalise same-sex marriage.

2004   Officials in California and Oregon start to issue wedding licences to same-sex couples, but public pressure forces a change back to illegal status.

UK recognises equal legal rights for same-sex couples and heterosexual couples joined in civil ceremonies.

2005   Spain, South Africa and Canada legalise same-sex marriage.

Pope John Paul calls same-sex marriage 'evil'.

2008   California overturns ban on gay marriage then bans it once more the following year – Proposition 8.

2009   Iowa, Vermont, Maine, USA, legalise same-sex marriage.

India declassifies homosexuality as a mental illness.

2010   New Hampshire, USA legalises same-sex marriage; Californian courts battle over the legality of Proposition 8.

Further information

Books:

Gay Marriage (Introducing Issues with Opposing Viewpoints)
Lauri Friedman, editor (Greenhaven Press, 2009)

Sexual Orientation and Society (Issues Series vol. 153)
Lisa Firth (Independence Educational Publishers, 2008)

Same-sex Marriage: Moral Wrong or Civil Right?
Tricia Andryszewski (Twenty-First Century Books, 2007)

Websites:

http://www.hrc.org/issues/5517.htm
The Human Rights Campaign site should answer your questions about same-sex marriage

http://www.tht.org.uk/
The Terrence Higgins Trust is the leading and largest HIV and sexual health charity in the UK and their website has lots of information about sexual orientation, choices and safety, including the publication 'Out in School'

http://www.eachaction.org.uk
Visit this site to find out about recognising and battling against homophobia at school and in other places

http://www.bbc.co.uk/archive/gay_rights/
Archive recordings and programmes from 1957 to the present about the evolution of gay rights in the UK

Index

Numbers in **bold** refer to illustrations